FAITH IN POLITICS

To my wife,
Finola

John Bruton

Faith in Politics

A collection of essays on politics, economics, history and religion

First published in 2015 by
CURRACH PRESS
55A Spruce Avenue,
Stillorgan Industrial Park,
Blackrock, Co. Dublin

Cover design by Helene Pertl/Currach Press
Origination by Currach Press
Printed by ScandBook AB, Sweden

ISBN 978 1 78218 841 4

This publication is protected under the Copyright and Related Rights Act 2000. Conditional to statutory exceptions, no part of this work may be reproduced without the express permission of Currach Press.

The moral rights of the author have been asserted.

Copyright © 2015, John Bruton

CONTENTS

	INTRODUCTION	VII
1.	IRISH POLITICS	1
2.	ECONOMY	31
3.	ENVIRONMENT	71
4.	HISTORY	85
5.	EUROPEAN UNION	125
6.	BOOK REVIEWS	171
7.	WORLD POLITICS	199
8.	RELIGION	219

INTRODUCTION

∽

This book was suggested to me by Currach Press. They had been following my blog since 2009 and, somewhat to my surprise, felt it could form the basis for a book.

I had been posting commentaries on the web on ongoing events since the late 1990s, initially while I was leader of Fine Gael in the form of daily messages on the Fine Gael website.

The discipline of looking back at meetings, discussions and visits, and committing my impressions to paper, helped me to crystallise inchoate thoughts and get the most out of the many valuable insights I was being offered by others.

When I became European Union Ambassador in Washington, I decided to do this by posting a weekly message, always written by myself personally, on the EU Delegation in Washington website, where they can still be accessed. None of these posts, nor any of the earlier Fine Gael messages, are included in this book.

On my retirement as Ambassador in November 2009, I decided to continue posting regular messages, this time on my own website, www.johnbruton.com. These post-2009 messages form the raw material from which this book has been compiled.

I wish to express my heartfelt thanks to Fearghal O'Boyle, Michael Brennan, Patrick O'Donoghue, Leeann Gallagher, Helene Pertl and Shane McCoy of Currach Press, and to my research assistant and daughter, Mary Elizabeth Bruton, for the immense amount of work they have done in editing, proofreading and suggesting improvements to the text.

Apart from the chapters on religious topics, many of the themes explored in this book reflect on areas for which I have had some official responsibility during my professional life.

Education, economic development, commerce, fiscal policy and energy policy were covered by ministerial portfolios I held in Ireland.

At European Union level, as a member of the Convention on the Future of Europe and later as EU Ambassador in the United States, I came to have a good understanding of why the EU is such a brave, ambitious, and also fragile project, and how its value needs to be explained to a public that is inclined to take it for granted.

As Taoiseach, I had to deal with the painfully slow process whereby the Irish Republican movement came to recognise that killing people was never going to bring a United Ireland – or even a good life – for the people whose cause they sought to espouse.

This led me to reflect on how misconceptions about history can distort how people deal with present realities, and on how national myths need to be rigorously questioned. This is a major theme in the book. Violence is all too easy to glorify. It simplifies what is complex. It forces people to take sides rather than to think things through. It is far too easy to develop a cult around those who died young, and to ignore what was achieved by those who lived, rather than died, for their country.

This has a particular relevance when the centenary of the violence of 1916, and of the period from 1919 to 1923, is to be elaborately commemorated. These commemorations are liable to mistakenly romanticise, and thereby vindicate in the public mind, the needless violence initiated in 1916.

The lesson of the 1966 commemorations, which preceded by only three years the pointless IRA campaign which lasted from 1969 to 1997, sadly has not been learned. The virtually complete neglect of centenaries of peaceful achievements, like the centenary of the passage into law of Home Rule on 18 September 2014, allows the commemoration of subsequent violent acts to get an undeserved, and unnecessarily high, profile.

If the passage into law of Home Rule had been commemorated with an equally high profile two years ago, people might have seen all the elaborate ceremonial around 2016 in a more thoughtful light; but that opportunity was lost.

In this book, I lay out the case for a proper celebration of the achievements of non-violent constitutional nationalism. The fact that Ireland remained a democracy in the 1930s and 1940s, when so many other new states lapsed into dictatorship, is an immense achievement of constitutional politics. It might not have been possible without an earlier achievement of constitutional politics – land reform – which gave so many more people a stake in the country and in its democratic order. These are the things modern Ireland should commemorate.

I hope this book also makes a good case for the profession of politics itself. As its title suggests, the book is an expression of my faith in democratic, constitutional politics.

At a time when both were held in much higher esteem than they are today, James Dillon said that politics is a vocation, second only to the religious life. I believe politics is a high form of public service, and while no politician is without fault, almost all who enter the profession do so from high motives.

Politics deals with the really difficult questions; questions that are too difficult to be left to scientists, to administrators or to courts. So it is inevitable that practitioners of politics will come in for disproportionate criticism. That is in the very nature of the unsettled issues with which they are dealing.

By the nature of their profession, politicians are generalists, in an age when other professions have become ever more narrowly specialised and have learned to think within administrative and legalistic silos. A politician's job is to ensure that the silos of modern society can converse with one another about the decisions that must be taken for the common good.

There seems to be a higher level of scepticism about politicians nowadays than at any time in my life.

This is partly because the problems of modern society, like maintaining a balance between finding money for health services and keeping tax at reasonable levels, are increasingly complex. Confronted with complexity, the simple approach – of blaming the politicians for not finding a pain-free solution – allows people to avoid having to do the arithmetic for themselves.

The negativity about politics has also come about because electorates are coming to realise that the conditions of post-war Europe, including rapid and almost continuous increases in living standards and of government revenues, were temporary and historically exceptional, and that, as our population ages, living standards may not continue rising.

The choices that will thus have to be made through the medium of democratic politics will become more, not less, difficult. One hopes that political institutions are strong enough to enable politicians and political parties to make these decisions in a timely fashion.

As explored in this book, the institutions for decision-making in some countries, for example the United States, seem ill-designed to make some categories of decision. Ultimately, political 'institutions' are not so much legal devices as habits of thought and action. As with individuals, states can also fall into bad habits!

Irish Politics

COALITION EXPERIENCE IN IRELAND – WHAT WORKS

During my political career from 1969 to 2004, there were five major parties in Irish politics, all of whom had some involvement in coalition governments at different times.

These were, in declining order of size:

- Fianna Fáil (a traditional nationalist party, which until 1989 had refused to take part in coalitions on principle),
- Fine Gael (a centrist party in the European Christian Democrat tradition),
- The Labour Party (Social Democrat party with trade union links),
- the Democratic Left (a socialist party since merged with the Labour Party) and
- the Progressive Democrat party (a party that espoused liberal economics which has since been wound up).

I served in four different coalition governments: 1973–7, 1981–2, 1983–7, and 1994–7. In addition to the coalitions in which I served during this period, there has also been a Fianna Fáil/Labour Party coalition (1992–4) and Fianna Fáil/Progressive Democrat coalitions (1989–92 and 1997–2002). Fine Gael and Labour had also participated together in coalitions in the 1940s and 1950s.

I was a junior minister in the 1973–7 coalition governments involving Fine Gael and Labour, a full cabinet minister in the second and third (1981–2 and 1983–7), and Taoiseach (Prime Minister) in the fourth one (1994–7).

All the coalitions in which I served involved my party, Fine Gael, as the largest party, and the Irish Labour Party, as the second largest. There was also a third party, the Democratic Left, in the 1994–7 government.

These are the main lessons I have derived from my experience.

Having a parliamentary majority is a big help
The parties in the 1981–2 government did not make up a majority in the Dáil (Parliament), hence the government's short life.

While it did obtain a majority vote for an emergency budget shortly after taking office in 1981, it could not persuade a majority to vote for its more comprehensive budgetary proposals in 1982. The result was a general election, which the government lost. They were succeeded by a minority Fianna Fáil government, which introduced a budget almost identical to the one they had voted against in order to bring down the previous coalition.

Having a majority is particularly important to coalition governments because internal negotiations between the coalition parties themselves tend to be difficult enough, without the added complication of negotiating with individual deputies, or parties outside the government, to ensure a majority to pass individual measures one by one. The unnecessary doctrine of budget secrecy adds to the difficulty because it creates a 'high noon' situation on budget night, when negotiation is impossible.

All the other coalitions, apart from the 1981–2 one, had working majorities for all business on which the parties could agree, but the 1983–7 coalition broke up because the parties could not agree between themselves on policy for the 1987 budget.

A third party in government can mitigate tensions
The 1994–7 coalition of three parties (Fine Gael, Labour and the Democratic Left), which I led as Taoiseach, was the only three-party government in Irish history formed in the middle of a parliamentary term without a general election.

A realignment of parties to form that new government without a general election was made possible by by-election victories for parties in opposition earlier in the parliamentary term. It was also necessitated by a breakdown in trust between the Labour Party and Fianna Fáil, with whom Labour had formed a coalition after the 1992 general election.

My personal opinion is that the dynamic of a three-party coalition is easier to manage than that of a two-party coalition. This is because, if there is a difference between two of the parties, the third one can often be the catalyst for compromise. The presence of three parties in the coalition can avoid binary conflicts on a given issue, where one or other of only two parties has to lose face.

The dynamic of coalitions will vary, depending on how they came about
The internal dynamic of each of the four coalitions in which I was involved was different. The personalities involved were different, and personality traits are very important in politics. But the circumstances of their election, and the relativity in size of the parties and economic conditions, also made a big difference.

The parties in the 1973–7 and 1994–7 governments remained united and faced the general elections of 1977 and 1997 respectively, seeking re-election on a joint programme. This is a testament to good relations between the coalition parties. In the other cases, the outgoing coalition parties contested the elections separately. To date, however, no coalition government of the same parties has been re-elected in the following election.

A coalition that agrees on a joint programme before the election from which it emerges, as was the case with the 1973–7 coalition, probably has a better chance of staying together for the full term, and seeking re-election on a joint programme, than has a coalition that has not negotiated and formed until after the election.

This is so for the following reason: if parties have fought an election on different and competing programmes, and subsequently have to negotiate a joint programme involving the inevitable sacrifice of points on which they had fought the election, this will make the subsequent life of the government more difficult. Such parties are more likely to be accused of 'broken promises'. But agreeing on a joint programme before an election, in which coalition parties will still be competing for votes with one another, is not easy either.

On the relative size of parties' representation
The 1973–7 Fine Gael/Labour government was elected on the basis of an agreed platform, which encouraged electoral co-operation between them and maximised their seats. The leaders of the two parties had experienced the frustration of opposition, having served in parliament for a long time, mostly out of power, and this made them personally determined to hold the government together, notwithstanding the substantial differences in interest between their support bases. Labour had a strong influence on the taxation policies of this government, which reflected the number of seats they had.

In the parliaments of the 1981–2 and 1983–7 periods, the Fine Gael party was numerically stronger, relative to Labour, than it had been in the 1973–7 period, and this had to be reflected in the content of the government's economic policy. Economic conditions were difficult because of international circumstances, and framing fiscal policy was thus a hard task. Labour influence was exercised to resist reductions in public spending, which inevitably increased the overall tax burden.

On economic circumstances
The three-party coalition of the 1994–7 period served in more benign economic times. Economic growth accelerated rapidly during the term of office of the government, which made the framing of fiscal policy easier than it had been in the 1980s.

While Fine Gael was the bigger party, Labour had more parliamentary strength than it previously had in the parliaments of the 1980s, and this additional strength was reflected in the fact that Labour held the Finance Ministry, a post that the bigger party had always held in previous coalitions. This ensured that there was a better sharing of responsibility for fiscal policy between the parties than may have been the case before, which reduced tension. The Democratic Left also played a key role in facilitating compromise, as indicated earlier.

On systems for managing inevitable differences
The 1994-7 government benefitted from having a more structured system for resolving policy differences between parties and ministries than had been the case in earlier coalitions.

Ministers from all three parties each had two advisors who were political appointees. One was a 'Programme Manager', whose job it was to work with his/her own minister and the other Programme Managers to ensure that the agreed programme of the three parties was implemented across government. The other appointee was a conventional political advisor who looked after his/her minister's political interests, relations with their party, etc.

In my view, the Programme Manager system was particularly effective in ironing out technical disputes on politically sensitive issues that had absorbed too much time and emotional energy at the cabinet meetings of previous coalitions.

As a general rule, as Taoiseach, I did not take an issue to cabinet unless differences had first been ironed out, or simplified, by the Programme Managers, or in discussion between the three party leaders.

On understanding a smaller party's difficult role
The relationship between a bigger and a smaller party in a coalition is a sensitive one because experience in Ireland has been that the smaller party tends to get more of the blame, and the bigger party more of the credit, for what the coalition does in government. Thus the smaller party runs the risk of doing relatively less well in the subsequent election.

Dealing with this problem is a primary responsibility of the leader of the bigger party, the Taoiseach of the day. To this end, in the 1994-7 coalition I minimised, to some extent, my own media appearances to allow attention to be taken by other ministers, including Labour ministers.

I also arranged for regular separate meetings of Fine Gael ministers where we discussed issues that might be coming up well ahead of time, with a view to identifying ways to manage any of them that might otherwise cause friction between the parties at the cabinet table.

One might have thought that separate meetings of this kind would create a 'them and us' situation, but in practice, the opposite was the case. These meetings allowed ministers with a perceived grievance about the other party to speak their mind to party colleagues rather than across the cabinet table, and thus gave time for such concerns to be addressed or put in better perspective in private discussion, without becoming a source of inter-party tension.

In my experience, the most corrosive thing that can happen to a coalition is the development of a practice of anonymous off-the-record briefings by, or on behalf of, ministers about what other ministers or the other party in government is doing. In these briefings, things may be said that would not even be said face to face across the cabinet table. This is worse than an open row because it destroys trust. It is incompatible with collective cabinet responsibility. Once it starts, it is difficult to stop, and it is often hard for anyone, including the Taoiseach, to pin down who is responsible for it.

Probably the best way to stop this is for it to be raised in regular separate meetings of ministers in each party, where better ways of dealing with whatever problem has prompted the off-the-record briefing can be identified and the practice stopped.

Looking to the future, it is likely that coalitions will be formed of parties that never coalesced before. The success or otherwise of such coalitions may depend on the deliberate cultivation of trust building institutions of the kind I have described here.

DIVIDED SOCIETIES —
HOW WILL THEY SURVIVE THE RECESSION?

Northern Ireland faces real economic threats. It is heavily dependent on the UK Exchequer. 32% of its workforce is employed in the public sector. This contrasts with 19% in the rest of the UK and 20% in the Republic of Ireland.

That large public sector in Northern Ireland is kept going by an annual net transfer of £16 billion from the UK Exchequer. But the UK Exchequer is running short of money. It has a budget deficit of 6.5%, and there are competing demands for money from different parts of the UK and from particular services, like the NHS, which tend to become more expensive as the population ages.

All major parties in the UK are agreed that there will have to be a severe restraint in spending by the UK Exchequer. Such cutbacks are proportionately more threatening the more dependent an area is on public-sector employment, as Northern Ireland is.

Is the Northern Ireland power-sharing system capable of making quick, fair and efficient decisions to reduce public spending in a timely way?
The long continuing difficulties of the parties in the Executive in finding a way for Northern Ireland to live within its available resources, notwithstanding the continuing subsidy from Westminster, is an example of the difficulty there is in having the normal politics of compromise in a political system where the parties are actually required to define themselves by, and on the basis of, two sets of completely irreconcilable aspirations: either the aspiration to a United Ireland outside the UK, or continued adherence to the UK.

The Good Friday Agreement requires that parties must register themselves as 'Unionist' or 'Nationalist' to exercise full voting rights in the complex voting/vetoing process by which Stormont makes decisions.

When the Good Friday Agreement was debated in the Dáil on 21 April 1998, I drew attention to these difficulties. I said: 'If the two communities continue to define themselves in ways that cannot be reconciled with one another, there will be difficulties in achieving the rapprochement sought by the Agreement between them. The Agreement itself contains a voting procedure that requires parties to designate themselves as adherents of one of two opposite aspirations. As long as the two communities define their very existence in irreconcilable terms, arguments on almost any topic that appeals to one community will tend to create fear in the other community.'

I argued that Northern Ireland would make progress if it replaced the politics of aspiration with the politics of accommodation. That has not happened. In fact, things are getting worse.

For a while, the aspiration of 'peace' was one that both communities could share and work towards. But once peace was achieved, and lives were no longer being lost, the communities tended to relax backwards into the comfortable certainties of championing their own side's concerns and ignoring those of the other side.

In 1998, I said: 'We must create a new common aspiration binding together Unionists and Nationalists in their common work. Without the emotional cement of common aspirations there is a real risk that the new institutions will revert to negative factionalism fed by constant reminders that the defining aspirations of the two communities are contradictory.'

That has not happened either. The crisis over the welfare reform package shows that 'negative factionalism' is the dominant feature in Northern Ireland politics.

Furthermore, symbolism is being used to reinforce division, and to reinforce and highlight the contradiction between the supposed 'aspirations' of the two communities.

On the one hand, councils where there is a Nationalist majority, but a significant Unionist minority, aggressively promote the use of place names in Irish and refuse to *ever* fly the Union Flag, as if people of the Unionist non-Irish-speaking tradition did not belong locally.

On the other hand, Unionist-majority councils will ignore the sensitivity of their Nationalist minority by insisting on flying the Union Flag 365 days of the year, as if to remind Nationalists of their minority status and of the fact that their aspiration has not been, and will not be, achieved.

Even commemorations which should be shared, like that of the Great War dead, who included people from both communities, are presented as one-sided events.

The fact that the Executive has most recently been brought to the brink over what should be an administrative matter, a disagreement on the cost implications of certain welfare changes, shows how deep the distrust is. This is not a disagreement between people who do not know one another, or who have not had opportunities to check the cost of different measures before they agree to them. The relevant passages from the Stormont House Agreement, agreed between the DUP and Sinn Féin, say:

- The (UK) government has developed a comprehensive financial support package to help the Executive deliver across its priorities. The total value of the government package represents additional spending power of almost £2 billion. Details of the financial package are in a financial annex attached to this agreement.

- A final balanced budget for 2015–16 needs to be agreed in January.

- Legislation will be brought before the Assembly in January 2015 to give effect to welfare changes alongside further work.

- Implementation of these welfare changes will begin to take place in the financial year 2015–16 and implementation will be complete by 2016–17.

Only monumental lack of ministerial competence can explain how specific agreements like this could be reached in December, only to unravel in March, without the party withdrawing from the deal (Sinn Féin) saying where the extra money it wants is to be found.

It is a disagreement between full-time ministers, with large full-time staffs, who have been ministers together in a shared administration for years, and who had negotiated about these precise matters in the Stormont House Agreement for weeks, and yet they say they had not worked out and agreed the cost of particular welfare changes!

In a normal system, such a failure by ministers would be regarded as incompetence warranting removal from office and replacement by the opposition. But the nature of the system is such that there is no opposition, and the choice is between the collapse of the Assembly and a restoration of direct rule, or a continuation of the present stagnant game.

Another issue that divides the parties is that of provocative parades. On this the parties agreed, in the Stormont House Agreement, that the governance of parades will be devolved from Westminster to the Northern Ireland Assembly, and that reasonable-sounding criteria be brought into law in new legislation on parades.

They agreed that regulation of parades and related protests should be based on respect for the rule of law, respect for those who parade, respect for those who protest, and respect for those who live and work in areas in which parades and protests take place.

The implementation of such legislation will be the test. 'Respect' is the key word here. But how much agreement is there between the parties on what respect requires? If respect for the other community is not shown by elected councils in the policy of flying flags on council buildings, how do they expect to reach a common definition of 'respect' when it comes to contentious parades?

One of the reasons for the lack of urgency in coming to agreements on difficult matters like these is that the power-sharing arrangements at Stormont mean that the Executive does not face an opposition that is ready to take over from it.

So long as each of the two bigger parties keep their supporters in their own 'community' happy, they are guaranteed their ministerial places and do not have to worry about what the supporters of parties from the other 'community' are thinking.

It also seems that competition from smaller parties on their own side, who have been required to define themselves in one camp or the other, often makes it more, rather than less, difficult for the big parties to compromise in a timely way.

These arrangements were, of course, put in place for understandable reasons and to deal with a historic problem.

In order to prevent a majority-take-all system coming about, as was the case in Northern Ireland from 1920 to 1972, when the Unionist majority had all the power, the 1998 Agreement required that every decision have the agreement of a sufficient number of both Unionist and Nationalist representatives.

This is what is called 'cross-community consent'. Each decision must, at minimum, have 40% support of representatives who have registered themselves formally as 'Unionist' and also 40% of those registered as 'Nationalist'. Representatives of parties who decline to register as either 'Unionist' or 'Nationalist' may vote, but their votes do not count when it comes to deciding if cross-community consent has been obtained for a particular decision.

Thus the votes of members of the Assembly who do not register in one of the two ancient camps are worth less than the votes of those who do.

This means there is a built-in disincentive to the formation of parties that strive to win support on the basis of providing a new politics that transcends the historic divisions, and a disincentive to vote for such parties too.

Because parties have an incentive to identify themselves exclusively with one community or the other, they tend not to bother to appeal for votes from the other side at all. Electioneering thus becomes a process of segmentation of the electorate, not of reconciliation of the electorate.

On a seesaw, weight applied at the extreme ends of the seesaw has more leverage than weight applied near the midpoint. Northern Ireland politics has worked on that same principle.

As the work of the Executive and the Assembly is a constant search for a balance between the weights of two narrowly defined communities, there is a tendency for electors to choose parties at the more extreme end of their own particular community spectrum, to maximise leverage for their side, or to counterbalance the election of extremists on the other side.

In fairness, it must be acknowledged that there might never have been an agreement at all in 1998, if these complicated, and apparently perverse, arrangements had not been put in place. And if there had been no agreement in 1998 a lot of people might have been killed in conflict since then.

But it is now time to accept that, while the arrangements have kept the peace, they have also preserved the divisions that led to the conflict in the first place. Now may be the time to start thinking about ways to achieve cross-community consent without artificially polarising representation in the way the present system does.

One might, for example, say that for any Executive to be formed, it must have the support of 75% or 66% of the Assembly, and that all decisions of the Assembly must have a vote of that percentage to go through. One could then cease requiring parties to register as 'Unionist' or 'Nationalist' for the purposes of establishing cross-community consent. Under Proportional Representation that would reward parties who seek the centre ground between the two communities in ways that the present arrangements do not.

But it would still, in practice, require cross-community consent, because no decision could assemble the required support without a lot of support in both of the two traditional 'communities'.

It is important to remember that even divided societies like Northern Ireland, Belgium, Macedonia and Lebanon will not always escape the need to make tough decisions to curb spending. They need systems that are robust enough to make decisions that are speedy as well as fair, and which promote a search for the centre ground, rather than a scramble for leverage at opposite ends of the spectrum.

The recent difficulties in Northern Ireland are the result of political opportunism, lack of courage, and incompetence; they also illustrate a wider design problem that needs to be studied by all those who want to build structures in other parts of the world that will reconcile divided communities while also providing effective and cost-efficient government.

IAN PAISLEY
SOME SAY RELIGION AND POLITICS SHOULD NOT MIX

One cannot fully understand Ian Paisley without understanding the biblical tradition from which he sprang. Calculation, religious conviction, and the changed perception of paramilitarism after 9/11 explain why Dr Ian Paisley eventually became 'Dr Yes', after having been 'Dr No' for so long.

As he approached the end of his life, Ian Paisley really wanted to be the man who was seen to have brought an end to the Troubles in Northern Ireland.

Not long before the eventual breakthrough on the issues of policing and power sharing, Ian Paisley had suffered a serious illness. He told Tony Blair, after he had recovered, that he had recently had a 'near meeting with his Maker' and added that he did not want to end his life being remembered as an old man who said 'no' to every proposal that might have brought a settlement.

He struck the same conciliatory tone in his final speech to the House of Commons. He said then that one must face the fact that the people of Northern Ireland are diverse, politically and religiously, and, as such, must find a way of living together. They were not a 'hard people', but a 'caring and a loving people'. He recalled that, in his youth, his province was a much more neighbourly place than it later became. Calm and peace were now being restored, he said, and the day would come, although he 'might not live to see it', when the Troubles would be forgotten.

How can this transformation of a man who stirred up so much animosity for over thirty years be explained?

How did someone who had campaigned for the rejection of the

Good Friday Agreement in the referendum of 1998 come to take office as First Minister under the same Agreement nine years later?

Of course, there was an element of political calculation. Once his party became the largest Unionist party, compromise was more attractive than it would have been if David Trimble were to be the principal beneficiary. Similar calculations explained Sinn Féin's change of heart once they became the biggest nationalist party. But I believe part of the explanation lies in Ian Paisley's recognition of his own mortality, and in an evolution of his own evangelical Protestant faith.

Long before he finally accepted the Good Friday Agreement, he had already modified his attitudes towards Catholics. For example, he had noisily denounced Pope John Paul II as an 'Anti-Christ' in the European parliament in 1988. But when the same Pope died in 2005, his words were warm and conciliatory, and very different from the bitter words he had spoken on the death of Pope John XXIII in 1963.

How might such a theological evolution have come about?

While living in the United States, I was told that President George W. Bush played a part in convincing Dr Paisley that there was a biblical justification for accepting an accommodation with nationalists. President Bush was someone who read the bible every day and could find the right authority there for a change of political course.

Ian Paisley's father, James Paisley, was a Baptist minister, and a signatory of Edward Carson's Ulster Covenant. Ian, born in 1926, followed him into religious ministry and trained in a school for evangelical ministers in Wales. Returning to Northern Ireland, he quickly became involved in politics. Before founding his own party, he was a member of an organisation known as the National Union of Protestants, headed by the Stormont MP Norman Porter. In 1966, he founded his own newspaper, *The Protestant Telegraph*, and the Protestant Unionist Party, the precursor of the DUP.

In this phase of his career he was vigorously anti-Catholic, in both the political and the religious sense. Yet, even then, he was always a good MP in the service of his Catholic, as well as his Protestant, constituents in North Antrim.

He was against any involvement of the Irish state in the governance of Northern Ireland, and this was why he opposed the

Anglo-Irish Agreement. But he was not averse to an internal settlement with Nationalists within Northern Ireland itself.

His reasoning here was one-sided. Just as his Unionist constituents would feel exposed and insecure in any arrangement that had no British dimension, northern Nationalists would have felt exposed and insecure in any arrangement that lacked an Irish dimension. Ian Paisley chose, for a long time, not to see that.

On other matters he was more clear-sighted. He once said that it would be 'naive to take the IRA at its word'. He was right. An organisation which had no scruples about taking life would hardly be scrupulous about the truthfulness of assurances it might give. Many chose, deliberately, to remain naive about the IRA, arguing – mistakenly in my view – that this served the cause of peace.

Two developments changed the argument.

9/11 utterly changed the attitude of Irish–Americans to all paramilitary organisations, while the Northern Bank raid, and other IRA atrocities like the McCartney murder, changed Irish Nationalist and liberal opinion. Even the IRA itself realised its previous position on arms decommissioning was untenable. On decommissioning, Dr Paisley could justly claim that others came around to his point of view, not the other way around.

When, in 2007, he eventually took office as First Minister, he was eighty-one years of age. When he retired as a member of the House of Commons, he was the oldest MP there.

I last met him when, as First Minister, he visited Washington in the company of his Deputy First Minister, Martin McGuinness, to promote investment in Northern Ireland. What struck me at the time was the genuine affection there seemed to be between the two men, although I do not think they had got around to actually shaking hands by then, if indeed they ever did!

Ian Paisley may have had a Scottish name, but he always struck me as a particularly Irish political figure. Perhaps it was the bombast that one could never take completely seriously. Perhaps it was the sense of humour. Perhaps it was the twinkle in his eye that seemed to belie the violence of his words.

As a politician, Ian Paisley was an artist rather than a scientist, a man who knew that one had to appeal first to people's emotions before engaging with their reason. He was a master of timing.

Like a lot of Irish politicians before him, he tried out a lot of wrong paths, before he eventually found the right one. But by the time he did find that right path, he knew for sure that he could bring his people with him. That is why he ended his long career on a high note.

I penned this obituary to Ian Paisley when he died in September 2014. I was actually in Hillsborough at a meeting of Co-operation Ireland when I heard the news. My text was subsequently published in the Irish Independent.

MARTIN McGUINNESS WENT TO WINDSOR

It is an anomaly that Martin McGuinness, Deputy First Minister of Northern Ireland and member of Sinn Féin, can manage to go to Windsor Castle to meet the Queen, but Sinn Féin MPs cannot bring themselves to vote and speak in a parliament to which they seek election.

Although Ireland and the United Kingdom have lived in peace beside one another since 1921, and have both been members of the EU since 1973, the 2014 visit of President Michael D. Higgins was, remarkably, the first state visit by an Irish Head of State to the United Kingdom.

The treaty of 1921, which brought the Irish Free State into existence, accepted the fact of continuing UK jurisdiction over Northern Ireland. The Irish constitution of 1937 also accepted this fact too, but asserted a right to reunification of the national territory to include Northern Ireland.

My understanding is that the existence of this territorial claim, which was not pursued in any serious way, was an obstacle in the minds of some Irish leaders to normal state-to-state relations. They seem to have felt that reciprocal state visits at head-of-state level (but not below that level) would have constituted full acceptance of UK jurisdiction in Northern Ireland.

This self-imposed and somewhat fastidious barrier was lifted in 1998 when the relevant Articles (2 and 3) in the Irish constitution were removed by a referendum vote of the Irish people. This was part of the package of measures that made up the Good Friday Agreement.

In Ireland, the coverage of the visit was enormous, and mainly focused on President Higgins and the Queen and their many visibly cordial interactions throughout the visit.

Unfortunately, in sections of the media in Britain, much attention was focused on the attendance of Martin McGuinness, a former member of the IRA and now Deputy First Minister of Northern Ireland, at the dinner in Windsor Castle. To my mind, it is totally unexceptional that Mr McGuinness would receive, and accept, such an invitation, given the office he willingly holds.

What remains exceptional is the fact that members of Mr McGuinness' party, Sinn Féin, put forward members to be elected as members of Parliament in Westminster who then refuse to take their seats there (although they maintain offices in the Palace of Westminster, and draw their pay and allowances there). If they attended and spoke in the House of Commons itself, they could work to affect the legislation that governs their constituents. That is what all other MPs do, no matter how much they disagree with one another.

It seems that, in some way, Sinn Féin do not attend and vote in the House – even though they do travel to London – because they do not accept the jurisdiction of the UK Parliament (although they are happy to receive and spend money raised and voted upon by that Parliament).

If that is the case, they are not honouring the will of the Irish people, who accepted the Good Friday Agreement in full, including accepting the principle of consent and the associated change in Articles 2 and 3 which involved a renunciation of any refusal to accept UK jurisdiction in Northern Ireland, until the people of Northern Ireland vote to join a united Ireland.

It is as if Sinn Féin, by their abstentionist stance, is simultaneously both accepting and rejecting the principle of consent. Perhaps they should study the creative approach to a similar dilemma taken by Éamon de Valera in 1927, when he found a way to take his seat in the Dáil.

Based on reflections published on my website in April 2014, after Irish President Michael D. Higgins had made a very successful state visit to Britain and was entertained by Queen Elizabeth II.

WHAT ARE IRELAND'S GOALS TODAY — ITS STRENGTHS AND ITS WEAKNESSES

∽

What are Ireland's goals today? Some may assume we simply want a restoration of Celtic Tiger conditions, of an economy growing at 8% a year, and of a herd-like pursuit of more property and of more conspicuous forms of consumption. However, I doubt whether many people really want to go back to those disorientating conditions. They did not bring us much contentment at the time and have not done much good for our bank balances since then.

Prosperity brought us more freedom and it allowed us to make far more new choices, both about what we could buy and about how and where we could live. But making choices is always hard work. Having to make too many choices at a time can actually make us discontented and stressed, which happened to some people in the Tiger era.

There is no sign, for example, that prosperity kept families together, or that there was less family breakdown, during the Tiger era than there was in earlier times when people had fewer options in their lives. A family break up brings a lot more pain than a pay cut.

I believe most people would prefer an Irish economy that was growing at a steadier pace than it was in the Tiger era; an economy growing at such a pace that would allow us more time as families and individuals to adjust to change, to understand what change does to us psychologically and spiritually, and to get our material and non-material priorities into a healthy relationship with one another.

A steady growth rate of around 3% to 4% should satisfy that criterion. It would allow us scope to devote about 1% of GDP to paying off personal and government debts and would leave 2% to 3% to improve living conditions and to put something aside for the extra costs we will have to meet after 2020, when the baby boomers have retired and we have a smaller workforce to support them.

A steady 3% to 4% growth rate is attainable. To achieve it, we must, as a society, look realistically at all our strengths, weaknesses, threats and opportunities. We must then set clear goals and make brave decisions to reallocate resources away from all uses that do not help us achieve those goals.

It should not be about what politicians promise us, because politicians are only promising us our own money anyway. It should be about what we can afford to promise ourselves. The biggest strength we have in Ireland is our human capital, the educated young workforce we have, some of whom were born here and some who have come here as immigrants. Their educational level is far above that of previous generations and we cannot afford to lose them to emigration. We need to keep their talent here.

Are we using them and their talents as well as we should? Are we sure they are not facing a closed shop when they look for work? Are the qualifications of immigrants being recognised, or is non-recognition of qualifications forcing them to work below their potential? If we have a negative answer to any of those questions, then there is a waste of human capital.

Human capital in our public service is not always used to the full. This is because there is too much hierarchy and duplication, and too many grades and layers of administration. The Irish public service wins much praise from foreign companies for its flexible problem-solving approach. We should build on that.

The Irish Health Service (HSE) is a big commitment of expensively educated talent. In addition to providing services today, it should become an innovator of saleable services and products. The application of information technology to giving medical care to the elderly, while they remain in their own homes, is an area in which Ireland should seek to become a world leader.

Our legal system also consumes vast human resources in ways that spend, rather than create, wealth. The emphasis on adversarial oral argument consumes talent and time in ways that greater use of written procedures would not, and foreign-trained lawyers find it hard to set up in practice here. More generally, the Irish system places heavy emphasis on legalistic process in areas like planning, refugee decisions and unfair dismissals. The result of all this 'process' is not fairer decisions, but simply slower and more expensive decisions. The Commercial Court is an example of how to do things better, where the system is designed to streamline the preparation for trial, remove unnecessary costs and stalling tactics, and ensure full pre-trial disclosure.

It is a matter of profound regret that the passage of the Legal Services Bill of 2011, which would improve the efficiency of our legal services, has been so much delayed. This delay has been criticised in several international reports on the Irish economy and has been blamed, rightly or wrongly, on lobbying by elements in the legal profession.

While the present generation is better educated than previous ones, there is room for improvement in Irish education. Not enough time is given in primary schools to foreign languages, science and maths, and too much is given to learning the two national languages. We should reallocate a couple of hours a week on the primary school timetable to science, maths and a foreign language.

Our universities are a huge talent bank, but they could do more. The criteria for advancement in academia may not coincide with what society would want for an Irish university, in this time of scarce resources. Universities may not do enough to promote new business development. Their teaching hours are often too short, and they could accommodate far more foreign students, especially if they operated a dual academic year system which would keep them operational all year round. Our visa system for foreign students should be streamlined.

The big multinational presence in Ireland is a huge source of strength. It has helped us change the way we think about business. Yet, individual entrepreneurship is vital too. Those who fail in business should be encouraged to start again. Instead, the appallingly heavy personal bankruptcy code in Ireland is an obstacle to entrepreneurship.

It has been reformed recently in the Personal Insolvency Act of 2012, but the new system has been criticised by some as not being particularly effective.

Critics of the operation of the law say that banks, who are obliged by new EU rules to meet more exacting capital ratios, are not willing to write down debts owed to them by an adequate amount to facilitate an agreement. It is difficult to generalise about this. Clearly no incentive should be given to those who refuse to co-operate with their banks, giving them concessions that are not offered to those who co-operate to the best of their ability.

Others say that the state, which is usually the priority creditor ahead of the banks, should also make a contribution by writing down some of the taxes and interest that may be owed to it.

There is a real conflict of interest here. The more banks write down the value of debts owed to them, the less they will be able to lend out to new borrowers. To the extent that banks are state owned, any debt write-off by banks is a write-off by the taxpayer. If, as part of a personal insolvency deal to allow someone to start back in business, tax arrears owed by that person were written off, this would mean a loss for the state, and would also be seen as unfair by other taxpayers who paid their taxes in full, even at the cost of personal hardship.

There would also be a constitutional issue if an attempt was made to retroactively change the value of securities and liens on property that lenders had negotiated to assure themselves they would be repaid. Retrospective legislation is always hazardous.

There is still a lack of credit for new Irish businesses, and that will remain the case as long as we rely on Irish lenders alone.

We should therefore systematically simplify our laws, at national and European level, to make it easier for banks from other countries to provide the credit direct to Irish consumers and businesses. That could mean harmonised EU laws on mortgages, bankruptcy, priority of creditors, etc. Until we do that we will not have an EU Banking and Credit Union.

Looking to agriculture, Ireland is an under-populated country with a lot of fertile land. The world population will grow by another three billion people by 2050 and all those people will have to be fed from a diminished global acreage of arable land. The way we use our fertile land in Ireland is not always the best possible. We depend too much on low-margin livestock production which produces methane and contributes to climate change. We need a new growth model for Irish agriculture. We need more young people to enter farming.

These are some of our strengths and opportunities, what of the threats and weaknesses?

The biggest weakness is superficial thinking – blaming others, pursuing scapegoats, waiting for something to turn up, producing unrealistic budgets, and thinking we can pass the buck.

The biggest threat is a panic in financial markets over Irish public finances, which, if it happened, would force the country into drastic adjustments that would cause a huge additional loss in our growth potential.

To mitigate these weaknesses, we need a credible fiscal plan for the next five years, whose assumptions and contingencies should be vetted in advance by the European Commission and the International Monetary Fund (IMF), both of whom would be wise to consult the opposition parties as well as the government as they go through the vetting process. This is, broadly speaking, the model that was adopted in the new rules concerning debts and deficits adopted by the EU for the Eurozone countries, and endorsed in the Fiscal Compact Treaty following a referendum (after the original version of this essay was written).

Based on reflections on the renewal of the Irish Republic, written in April 2010. These words were written at a time when Ireland was suffering the combined effects of the banking crisis and the collapse of the public finances because of the disappearance of property-related tax revenues. I have updated these reflections somewhat to take account of developments since then.

A TRIBUTE TO DR GARRET FITZGERALD

Garret FitzGerald, former Taoiseach, who died in May 2011, will forever stand out as a man who changed Ireland.

He changed our attitudes to the Northern question, helping us to see it as a matter of people and their allegiance and how these can best be respected, and no longer simply as a matter of territorial claim and counterclaim.

He changed attitudes to Europe, seeing that Ireland would do best in Europe if it contributed creatively to both the goals and ambitions of other members within the EU, and to achieving closer union, rather than focusing exclusively on our own needs and what we could extract from common funds.

Fluent in French and Spanish, he was enthusiastic about all the good things we shared with our fellow Europeans.

Although his primary degree was in languages, his doctorate was in economic planning, and he had a new and optimistic approach to economics. He believed that if problems were researched and analysed properly, they could be solved by public and private sectors working together in a planned way.

As a journalist, he continued to enlighten, entertain, and sometimes challenge his readers right up to the end of his life.

He was always interested in the opinions of people younger than himself, but did not conceal his own convictions.

I first got to know Garret FitzGerald when I was one of his students in UCD. Garret lectured us on his great interest, economic statistics. He convinced all of us that the available statistics were a greatly underused resource for those who wanted to understand what was going on in the Irish economy.

Around that time I also joined the Fine Gael party as a member in Dunboyne and of the Students Branch in Dublin. That also brought me into contact with Garret, who had recently been elected as a Fine Gael senator. The mother of one of my friends, David Clarke, was a close relative of Garret's late wife, Joan, so I got to know Garret socially, as well as through politics and his academic work.

What struck me most forcibly at that time was his relentless enthusiasm and optimism.

He was often criticised for speaking too fast and writing sentences that were too long. But these supposed faults were really just an indication of a man who felt that there was so much to do, and so little time in which to do it.

As a student of economics, I also found his regular articles in *The Irish Times* to be very helpful in relating the insights of economics to the practical problems of the day.

Another thing that struck me was his tremendous enthusiasm for Ireland taking its place in what was to become the European Union. He was active in committees studying the preparedness, or lack of preparedness, of different sectors of our economy for the stiff competition they would face in a free trade area with Britain and with the rest of Europe.

He strongly supported the work of the then government, and of the Fine Gael leaders of the time – James Dillon and Liam Cosgrave – in pursuit of Ireland's application to join the European Common Market.

He also had a very good understanding of the way the politics of a united Europe would work for a small country like Ireland. I remember him telling me many times that Ireland could do best in Europe if it was able to identify its interests with the interests of Europe as a whole.

Ireland needed to use its ingenuity to find a way of formulating what it wanted as part of a proposal that met a wider need. In the same spirit, he strongly supported the central role of the European Commission as the body that could find a synthesis of the interests of all members, and he was opposed to inter-governmental deals, which tended to serve only the big countries.

Garret was a very successful Minister for External Affairs in the coalition government led by Liam Cosgrave (1973–7). He energised the Irish Foreign Service and collaborated closely with Liam Cosgrave in framing the Sunningdale Agreement.

This agreement, negotiated in 1973, provided the template for the eventual settlement reached in 1998 in the Good Friday Agreement. It is such a pity that so many had to die before the Sunningdale model was finally accepted by the entire spectrum of Unionists and Nationalists in both parts of Ireland.

Garret FitzGerald became the leader of Fine Gael in the aftermath of the 1977 Election. The party had lost numerous seats and was facing the prospect of a long and demoralising period in opposition. It was entirely characteristic of Garret FitzGerald that he was not prepared to settle for that.

Few displayed as much energy as Garret FitzGerald did in reviving the fortunes of the Fine Gael party in the period between 1977 and 1979. It was due almost entirely to his leadership that the party was able to achieve such good results in 1979 local and European elections. This set the scene for Fine Gael's success in the 1981 general election.

I became the Minister for Finance in the government that Garret formed after that election. We faced a truly awful financial situation. With the support of Labour ministers, we prepared, introduced and passed a supplementary budget within barely one month of taking office. This speed was critical in maintaining Ireland's creditworthiness.

Subsequently we introduced, again with the full and informed agreement of both parties in the government, a budget for 1982 in January of that year. The government did not have a majority in the Dáil and had no permanent pacts with independent deputies, so there was a high risk that the budget might not pass the Dáil.

The choice was clear; we could either do what we believed was necessary, whatever the electoral consequence, or temporise and succumb to our problems.

Without hesitation, Garret chose the former course and the measures in that budget were largely implemented by the subsequent government.

The Anglo–Irish Agreement, which he negotiated with the support of Peter Barry and Dick Spring, was a crucial milestone on the road towards a more constructive relationship between Nationalism and Unionism on the island.

In government in the 1980s, when we needed to check public spending growth, Garret was always insistent on maintaining spending on education because of its lasting benefit, and this priority was crucial in laying the ground for growth in the 1990s.

One of the highlights of my time in Washington as EU Ambassador was when Garret and his granddaughter came to dine. He kept the guests, Irish, British and American, magnificently entertained with a constant stream of anecdotes, opinions and self-caricatures.

Ever an optimist, he continued working right up to, and through, his final illness. Although he eventually ceased to have a party affiliation, he continued to encourage politicians of all parties when they worked in what he saw as the national interest.

Economics

GLOBALISATION IS NOT SOMETHING THAT IS DONE TO US – IT IS SOMETHING THAT REFLECTS OUR CHOICES

Ireland's then new Minister for European Affairs, Paschal Donohoe TD, gave an interesting speech in October 2013.

He made the point that globalisation, of which many people complain, is not something 'done to us, but is a consequence of the human desire to communicate, share, and exchange'.

He is right.

He could have added that humans also want a lot of variety and choice in their lives, sometimes to an excessive degree, and that this drives globalisation forward as people go to the ends of the earth to find elusive 'highs' in their lives. He went on to say that the European Union gives us an opportunity to 'positively mediate the consequences of globalisation'. He is right here too.

A small country on its own, like Ireland, could have little impact on global trends, but the EU, as a block, can make a difference. Acting together, Europeans can have more influence on global forces than they ever could as twenty-eight separate countries acting on their own.

Globalisation has been facilitated by the Internet, containerisation, cheap air fares, and plentiful energy sources. All these took investment to generate, and would not have happened if people did not want them or were unwilling to pay for them. These technologies cannot be 'uninvented' now, so globalisation cannot be reversed. It is here to stay.

How should we cope with the consequences of globalisation?
All this variety, all this communication, and all this exchange, does not necessarily make us happier. In fact, the more choices we have to make, the more discontented we can often become. This is especially so if we feel we have to make these choices to keep up with neighbours, or others with whom we feel we must compare ourselves.

Choices are hard to make. They require an effort. They involve saying 'no' as well as 'yes'. And the more choices we have, the more things we have to say 'no' to. The more options we have, the more regrets we may have about the choices we made. The more choices we have, the more we expect of life, and of ourselves.

The Paradox of Choice, by Barry Schwartz, had the subtitle 'How the Culture of Abundance Robs us of Satisfaction'. People are shopping more nowadays, but enjoying it less. Increased choice may actually contribute to the recent epidemic of clinical depression. Depression has tripled in the last two generations, despite all the treatments now available, which were not there sixty years ago.

The culture of 'more choice' undermines institutions, like churches. Because choice is the priority, people do not want to regard religious teachings as commandments, but as suggestions about which they themselves are the ultimate arbiters.

The overestimation of the value of choice may also be a contributing factor in the increased divorce rate, because, as Schwartz puts it, 'establishing and maintaining meaningful social relations requires a willingness to be bound and constrained by them'. But constraints are exactly what the ideology of choice rejects.

Europe needs a renewed value system, if it is to mediate globalisation
'Studies have estimated that losses have twice the psychological impact as equivalent gains,' says Schwartz. In other words, people hate losing €100 a lot more than they like winning €100.

The more people have, the more they have to worry about losing. This may explain why people in modern, well-off societies are so anxious, and why, in the face of recent economic losses, many are regressing to old dead-end ideas, like nationalism, class warfare and xenophobia.

Happiness, as well as the Gross Domestic Product, is at last being measured by economists, and it seems that once a society's per capita wealth crosses a threshold from poverty to adequate subsistence, further increases in national wealth have little effect on happiness. You may find as many happy people in Poland as in Japan, even though the average Japanese person is much richer than the average Pole. This should make us stop and think.

Economic growth is a good thing, but it has physical limits, as we are discovering with climate change and pollution. Economic growth also has psychological limits, in the sense that some forms of growth increase anxiety by offering people a bewildering array of choices that they do not feel competent to make. Markets only work well if people are informed enough and have the time and mental energy to make wise choices.

Societies need a strong value system if they are to be happy. These values must put human respect ahead of material things, and put human relations ahead of maximising choice. The science of economics is only beginning to recognise this.

If the European Union is to positively mediate the consequences of globalisation, it must ask itself whether the values of more choice and more material abundance, both imported from economics, are sufficient to build a good society.

PORTUGAL AND IRELAND
– EXITING BAILOUTS, BUT DIFFERENT CHALLENGES

Ireland and Portugal are two Atlantic nations that both look west, rather than east.

In the fifteenth century, and long thereafter, Portuguese navigators invented, and promoted, globalisation. Portugal had trading posts in the Middle East, India, China and Indonesia as well as a large empire in Africa and South America.

Since the nineteenth century, Irish people, as emigrants, have been residents of every continent.

During my time in the United States as EU Ambassador, I became aware of the huge Portuguese influence there, in places like Rhode Island and Newark, New Jersey, both of which also happen to be among the most Irish places in North America.

Are there any lessons Ireland and Portugal can learn from one another as to how we found ourselves in need of EU/IMF bailout assistance, and how to move away from needing such help?

Both countries have had to use such loans to bridge the gap between government spending and revenue, because they could not borrow enough elsewhere. Like any bank manager of a client who is spending more than his income, the EU/IMF has imposed conditions which are difficult. In that sense, the EU/IMF has taken the blame for decisions that would have had to be taken anyway.

Ireland's debt/GDP ratio in 2014 was 114%, having fallen from 125%. Portugal's ratio was 131%. The big difference is the relative income of the people. The average per capita income in Portugal is about $21,000 per head, whereas the average in Ireland is $50,000 per head. In fact, Portugal is considerably poorer than the other bailout countries. Average wage rates in Portugal are only 75% of the level in Greece, and 66% of the level in Spain.

Some adults in Portugal have nothing at all to live on, and have to rely on family networks. Welfare, of some kind, covers almost everyone who needs it in Ireland, and basic welfare rates in Ireland have been preserved from cuts, notwithstanding the big fall in the revenues from which they must be found.

While 10% of Irish adults receive Lone Parent Allowances or some other form of social assistance from the state, only 4% of Portuguese adults do. Incidentally, the figure is only 4% in the UK as well, and most UK welfare benefits are paid at much lower rates than in Ireland.

One of the reasons Ireland has regained the confidence of lenders is the performance of its exports. Exports are the equivalent of 100% of Ireland's GDP, whereas Portuguese exports come to only 45% of its GDP. But Portuguese exports are rising faster than Irish exports. Portugal is catching up.

In the 1999 to 2007 period, Ireland's exports grew at the third fastest rate in the Eurozone (after Germany and Luxembourg), and Portugal had the seventh fastest. But in the 2007 to 2013 period, Portugal jumped to second place after Spain, and ahead of Germany. Ireland, notwithstanding its high absolute level of exports, fell back into sixth place. Ireland's slowing rate of export growth may be related to some of the pharmaceuticals it exports going off patent and thus becoming less valuable.

Portugal is a leading player in nano technology, but some say its strong exports are partly due to the diversion to exports, of goods that would have previously been sold in the, now depressed, home market.

Portugal has a well-developed infrastructure: it has twice as great an area of motorway per 1,000 people as the EU average, and has to spend 1.3% of its GDP on road maintenance, as against 0.9% in Ireland.

Portugal's economy grew very slowly from the early 1990s, and it continued to spend a little more than it was earning, gradually getting itself into the position it is in today. In contrast, Ireland's economy grew exceptionally quickly from 1995 to 2002, and then, in the short space of three years, developed a huge credit bubble, which burst in 2008.

In short, Ireland's problems were dramatic, Portugal's were chronic.

Both Ireland and Portugal suffer from remoteness from the centre of Europe. Portugal is cut off from the rest of Europe by its bigger, richer neighbour, Spain. Ireland has Britain, and the sea, between it and the continent.

So, why is Ireland relatively better off at the moment?

Portugal has an older population. As a result, Ireland spends half as much, as a proportion of its GDP, on pensions as Portugal does. On the plus side, life expectancy has dramatically improved in Portugal in recent times, by 8.5 years since 1980. During the 1970s, when Ireland, already an EU member, was laying the foundation for the Celtic Tiger by investing in technological education and promoting foreign investment, Portugal was in the midst of a revolution.

The conservative regime of Antonio Salazar was replaced by a junta of left-wing officers, who promoted a constitution which conferred all sorts of rights on people without creating commensurate resources, or responsibilities, to meet the cost of these rights. That constitution continues to inhibit the elected government to this day, preventing it from reducing expenditure to the level of the revenue it can raise without doing damage to the fabric of the economy.

The revolution also meant the abandonment of a costly colonial war and the return to Portugal of 600,000 descendants of former colonists, equivalent to 6% of the home population, all of whom had to be housed, fed and retrained for a new life. This diversion of resources delayed Portugal's modernisation at a crucial moment, and the country has never really caught up since.

The OECD (Organisation for Economic Co-operation and Development) has said that 'human capital is the Achilles' heel of the Portuguese economy'. Only 60% of Portuguese 25- to 34-year-olds completed second-level education, whereas 100% in Korea, 90% in Ireland, and 75% in Italy have done so. Too many Portuguese students have to repeat grades, rather than get the remedial help they need. Many of the qualifications of young Portuguese are not 'work relevant' according to the OECD. This is why Portugal has been forced to compete for low-wage work with countries in Eastern Europe, rather than move up the value chain to higher skill jobs, as Ireland has done.

But this is not something that can be remedied quickly. Ireland did not derive the full benefit from the educational changes made in the 1960s and 1970s until the 1990s.

Quicker gains can be made through reforms in the labour market. Wage rates and employment rules are set centrally in Portugal, whereas Ireland allows more freedom to negotiate at the level of the firm.

'Last in, first out' is a legal requirement in Portugal, regardless of the needs of the firm. The constitutional court has tended to protect the privileges of permanent and public sector workers, and this makes it difficult for Portugal to shift people and resources from the non-traded, protected sector of its economy to the export sector.

Like Ireland, Portugal has a problem of hardcore long-term unemployment. One in five children in Ireland grows up in a home where no one is working. This is building up a huge financial and psychological burden for the future. Ireland and Portugal could usefully compare notes on how to solve this problem.

Revenue collection is an area where Portugal could learn from Ireland. Self-assessment and intelligent use of computerisation and the Internet have enabled Ireland to reduce the cost of tax collection for taxpayer and government alike.

Getting government itself to function in a cohesive fashion is a problem everywhere. Different Ministries tend to develop their own empires, with their own mindsets. Communication, let alone coordination, between them is often difficult and interdepartmental committees are often ineffective. The Cabinet Secretariat of the current Irish government has been recommended to Portugal as a good example of how to tackle this problem.

Another area in which Portugal may benefit from studying what has been done in Ireland is the reform of the courts system. Delays and unpredictability in court decisions can be a major deterrent to foreign investment and a big cost for domestic businesses that are trying to grow. Court reform, initiated during my time as Taoiseach in the 1990s, has introduced computerisation, active case management and a specialised Commercial Court, all of which have been a big help.

As in Ireland, the current Portuguese government has been implementing a restructuring programme that was drawn up and agreed with the EU/IMF by its predecessor. This means that, in crude political terms, both governments can pass responsibility for what they have to do to both the EU/IMF, and to their respective predecessors in government.

Of course, to do so may mislead people to some extent, because the real driver of restructuring is not the EU, the IMF or the previous government, but a simple lack of money, a gap between spending and revenue, which is there anyway. It would be there no matter who was in power, and no matter who one was borrowing from.

Voters probably understand quite well that restructuring will continue in both countries long after the EU/IMF troika have gone. This will certainly be the case until the debt/GDP ratio is down to 60%, a figure both countries have agreed to in the Fiscal Compact Treaty.

Getting the ratio down to 60%, as the Irish people decided to do in a referendum on the Fiscal Compact Treaty, will mean running budget surpluses for many years, perhaps in the face of pressure to spend more or tax less. Continued restructuring is necessary for the simple reason that, if you want to borrow new money, you must repay old debts, and you must get your debts down to a manageable level.

When it comes to dealing with the problems of countries which have got into funding difficulties, I believe German, Dutch and Finnish people need to understand that an approach of doing as little as possible at the last possible moment carries extra costs.

These countries need to do some long-term thinking and devise systems that will create a robust structure of support and confidence for the Eurozone. For example, a conditional facility to issue Eurobonds, if agreed in principle, could give a big boost to confidence. Likewise, increasing the size of ESM funds to a market-intimidating size would increase the likelihood that they might not ever have to be used at all in practice.

Turning back to Portugal, what is the best way to build a truly sustainable economy?

I would suggest three themes, drawn from Irish experience.

Portugal should aim to make itself the best place in the world to set up a new business. Thanks to the Internet, a small business can become a global player much earlier in its life than was possible ten years ago. Portugal should make it easy to set up a new business, easy to enter a new profession and easy to comply with regulations.

Portugal should seek to identify new synergies between technologies and industries already in the country. Successful new business is not always about a new technological breakthrough, but about making new connections between existing technologies, or people, that have not been combined before. It is easier to build on existing strengths than it is to start something completely new. Existing Portuguese businesses should aim to become innovation communities, forming new partnerships and synergies in fields where their expertise can be more widely applied.

Finally, the global Portuguese community, many of them recent emigrants, can form a network that can bring business ideas and investments home to Portugal. Connect Ireland is a model Portugal could look at in this respect.

Based on a speech given in May 2013 at an economic conference in Estoril.

THE SOCIAL BENEFIT TO IRELAND, AND TO THE WORLD, OF IRELAND'S INTERNATIONAL FINANCIAL SERVICES INDUSTRY

Service is the key word
The financial service industry would not exist if its sole purpose was to provide jobs for those employed in it, and its consequential revenue to the state.

Like any other institution, the financial service industry exists because it is socially useful.

Before jobs or taxes, the industry exists to serve society and to meet the real needs of real people.

Of course, some participants in the industry have done things that were not consistent with social benefit. Sometimes they have spoken about their business to the rest of society in such impenetrable jargon, or with such condescension, that the social goals and benefits of financial services have been completely obscured from public view.

As President of IFSC (International Financial Services Centre) Ireland, my job is to promote Ireland as a location for new financial service activities. I put the emphasis on the word 'service'. The industry exists here to provide a service to the rest of the world. If it fails to provide a good service, the business will go elsewhere.

Ireland can provide these services to global customers better than any other country in the world.

Helping people mitigate the risks of life
The basic social goal of the Irish financial services industry is to help people all over the world make financial provision in the most efficient way – to mitigate the risks of life.

In some countries, people mandated the state to cover these risks for them. But as society ages, many states will have less and less fiscal capacity to cover all the risks they were able to cover when the working-age population was bigger and the elderly population smaller. Families all over the world will find themselves having to do more of the risk management for themselves. That is where the skills deployed by the professionals in the Irish international financial services industry will come into play.

The Irish international funds industry, for example, invests savings generated by pension contributions, and does so in such a fashion as to ensure that when people can no longer work for a living, they will have a pension.

That requires spreading money around different types of investment, so that risks of one type of investment are hedged by other investments.

Spreading investments to avoid vulnerabilities requires skills
Unlike what happens when people put money into shares in a particular company, or putting it all in just one bank, putting money into a fund that invests in different activities makes sure people do not have all their pension eggs in one basket. Different funds, and different investment strategies, will be tailored to different purposes.

An insurance company must ensure it always has money available to pay big claims if there is bad weather or some other such one-off, unexpected episode. In contrast, an investment for a pension fund will aim at having a steady flow of income. An investment to cover the cost of education will require a different strategy to one to cover end-of-life nursing care.

The skill of the financial service professional lies in understanding the needs of the client, and tailoring the mix of investments to get the right return, over the right time frame, with the right mix of risk and reward. The Irish industry can provide those skills. It can also look after the administration of the funds, enabling the asset managers to focus on what they do best.

Renewing global infrastructure and filling the lending gap
Another social need met by the financial service industry is that of assembling finance for the building and renewing of the world's infrastructure of roads, airports, rail links, electricity generation and distribution systems. Here the investor expects no return in the short run, but big and steady returns in the long run. This sort of investment is ideal for pension funds.

The contraction of the European banking system, because of past mistaken lending in the property sector, has created opportunities for other types of finance to enter the market and fill the gap in the provision of credit for business and house purchase.

Some of the capital of pension funds and insurance companies can, if supported by innovative intermediaries, be used to meet the social need for finance for home and business working capital. Irish innovation can play a role here in meeting both local and global needs and in filling the gap in the market left by the necessary contraction of traditional banks.

Technology to improve convenience
Another social goal the Irish financial services industry should aim to meet is that of extending the convenience of a banking service to people who still have to rely disproportionately on cash.

A technology centre in the Digital Hub in Dublin has been established to link innovators in the Irish software industry, where we are a world leader, with the international financial sector, where we are also a world leader. The aim is to use the most sophisticated information technology to extend banking services to a wider public, as well as complying with necessarily complex rules introduced since the financial crisis.

The application of technology can also help identify gaps in the market by using the skills in data analytics that exist in this country.

Finding out why the crisis really happened is the only way to avoid another crisis in the future
We must also apply our talents to ensure that the financial and banking crisis, from which we are slowly re-emerging, never happens again.

Asset bubbles and financial crashes have been part of human history since the invention of money. To mitigate bubbles and crashes, we must truly understand why and how they happen.

As the Nobel Prize-winning economist Robert Shiller said in his recent book, *Finance and the Good Society*: 'As much as Wall Street had a hand in the crisis, it began as a broadly held belief that housing prices could not fall – a belief that fuelled a full blown social contagion.'

He was speaking of the United States, but he could have been talking about Ireland. In other words, he was asking why people came to believe something that was fundamentally unbelievable, namely that house prices could only go upwards and not downwards. He went on: 'Learning how to spot bubbles and deal with them before they infect entire economies will be a major challenge for the next generation of finance scholars.'

He could have added a major challenge for 'finance practitioners and politicians'.

Ireland needs to apply its best brains to understanding the psychology of our recent bubble, to preventing this infection happening again. Only thus can we prevent a future one.

The task is not so much about apportioning blame – that's the easy bit – it is about understanding why people came to believe what they believed during the bubble. Unfortunately perhaps, no country is better positioned to provide that understanding of recent history than Ireland is. Doing so would be conferring a social benefit on the world.

Six thousand extra jobs since 2008, and over two billion in revenue to the state each year
In 2009, 29,704 people were employed in the Irish international financial services. By 2012, according to Department of Finance figures, the number of jobs had risen to 35,698.

The taxes paid by the industry have risen commensurately. The estimated tax contribution of the international financial services industry to the Irish Exchequer is €2.1 billion, equivalent to two-thirds of the entire voted capital budget of the state, or to 10% of the entire Social Protection budget.

Sometimes it is helpful in seeing the value of something by posing the counterfactual – where would we be if we had no international financial services industry? We would have almost 36,000 fewer jobs and would have to make a €4 billion budget correction next year, rather than a €2 billion one.

But it is only possible because our financial services industry provides a service that shrewd professionals all around the world are prepared to pay good money for. And they are only prepared to do that because this industry provides a good service, a social benefit, to its clients.

Apart from jobs and taxes, what other benefits does the Irish financial services industry confer on Ireland itself?

The Irish international financial services industry internationalises our country, bringing young people from all over the world to work here, and creating new opportunities for spin-off businesses.

It also regionalises our country, bringing high-quality jobs to places like Limerick, Carrick-on-Shannon, Navan and Naas, thus relieving congestion in the capital.

Based on a speech given in May 2014, when I spoke in Dublin as President of IFSC Ireland.

THE SOURCE OF ECONOMIC SUCCESS IN THE TWENTY-FIRST CENTURY: EACH COUNTRY WILL HAVE TO RELY ON ITS CHILDREN'S SKILLS AND INGENUITY IN AN INCREASINGLY COMPETITIVE WORLD

A lot of attention is being given to the competition Europe and the United States will face from economic growth in Asia over the next twenty-five years. A survey conducted by the World Economic Forum shows that Asia is the part of the world most optimistic about its economic future. And optimism is essential to investment.

The OECD has estimated that between now and 2060 GDP per capita will increase eightfold in India, and sixfold in Indonesia and China, whereas it will merely double in OECD countries, which include those in Europe and North America. This will affect the balance of power in the world. It is interesting to note that two of the top three Asian dynamos are democracies: India and Indonesia.

The source of economic growth can be summed up in two words: innovation and population.

Unblocking Europe's arteries to release innovation
If a country has an innovative and well-educated population, open to trends in the global market, able to understand them and identify the needs of the world, and an economic and governmental structure that allows speedy allocation of resources to meet those needs away from less efficient uses, it will have a higher growth rate.

This is why there is so much emphasis on 'structural reform' in OECD, IMF and EC advice to countries. Structural reform is designed to clear the arteries of the economy to allow blood to flow more quickly to the activities that will yield the best return.

For example, if a country has a disproportionately expensive, slow or overly elaborate legal system, that will be a blockage in the arteries. If a country has disproportionately high electricity prices because it uses electricity prices to subsidise uneconomic generation for regional policy purposes, that will block arteries. Likewise, if it has disproportionately costly or slow broadband communications, avoidable skill shortages, unwillingness to recognise genuine foreign qualifications, work disincentives for particular groups, or a distorted market for credit that does not favour productive activities, all these things are blockages in a country's economic arteries.

Such blockages can also apply at supranational level too. It has been estimated that the lack of a single market for digital services in the EU is blocking the arteries of the EU economy to the tune of €260 billion. Furthermore, the lack of a true single financial market is doing so to the extent of €60 billion, the lack of an integrated energy market to the extent of €50 billion, and the lack of a single services market (including non-recognition of skills certified in other countries) is blocking the arteries of the European economy to the extent of €235 billion.

Interestingly, a European parliament staff paper shows that one of the slowest countries to implement the structural reforms urged by heads of EU governments since 2011 is Germany. And one of the fastest, on paper at least, is Greece. These are reforms that Germany's own Chancellor recommended, along with her colleagues. One of the problems, in Germany's case, is the delays and resistance to change at the level of the lander (states) that make up the Federal Republic.

To put it all another way, Europe has a choice. According to the EU Ageing Report, the EU can stay on its present course, and, as in the last twenty years, have a total productivity growth rate of only 0.8% per annum, or it can make changes which could lift its total productivity growth rate to 1.1% per annum up to 2020 and 1.4% per annum thereafter. A slow, long-term return perhaps, but a real one all the same.

Structural reforms have differing potential between countries
Some countries, not Ireland, have been artificially held back by top-heavy bureaucracy that prevents their societies from allocating resources to where they will get the best return.

Societies can fail to best allocate resources, or block good reallocation of resources, by political vetoes and constitutional limits. Over-elaborate federal systems, like in Germany and the US, can also be a blockage to necessary change.

The reforms necessary include reforms to the labour market, but to a much greater extent they involve freeing up markets for the sale of goods and services – from electricity, to professional services, to government services – as I have mentioned already.

Of course, freeing up the arteries will not solve the problem unless there is a blood flow of commercial innovations based on good research and development, accompanied by an innovative and flexible culture within government, educational institutions and in the general population.

One can pour money into research in universities and yet fail through the lack of a fleet-footed innovative culture that would convert the results into globally saleable services and goods.

Between now and 2060, according to the OECD, the countries with the biggest upside potential for extra growth that might come about as a result of the implementation of structural reforms are China, Slovakia, Poland, Greece, India, Indonesia, Italy and Russia.

At the other end of the scale, some countries that already have relatively efficient systems are getting the benefit of reforms made in the past. These countries include the UK, the Netherlands, Ireland and the USA.

It is good that Ireland is in that position. This is an indication that the reforms we made over the last forty years or more have yielded fruit. And this is despite the fact that Ireland still has, to a degree, many of the rigidities I mentioned earlier, and has room to further improve in those areas.

But look at it another way – competitor countries, who have not yet made the obvious reforms, like China, Poland, Slovakia and Greece, have even *more* room to improve, or more upside potential, than we do, and may thus pose a bigger challenge to us, as soon as – or *if* – they get their act together.

Already comparatively efficient countries, like Ireland, the Netherlands, the USA and the UK, will have to look beyond structural reforms on their own if they are to make extra gains. They will have to run faster and faster just to hold their current relative position.

Structural reforms alone are not enough; the number of young people will make a key difference

In every society young people are the innovators. The crucial determinant of relative success in the twenty-first century between countries will be the proportion of young people in a country, and the relative mental agility of those young people, in comparison to those in other countries.

Their potential will be influenced by formal education, but not only by education. It will also be influenced by what happens to them as children, before they ever go to school.

Other things being equal, a country with a large elderly and middle-aged population is unlikely to produce as many innovators as a country with a large youth population. It is also likely to have more political veto points. Older electorates do not like change, even changes that may increase overall wealth in the long run. We have seen that in Germany, but not only there.

To an extent, each society decides the sort of future it wants to have when it decides how many children it will have.

Societies in many European countries, including Germany, Spain, Italy and many Eastern European countries, have decided to have few children. Partly as a consequence of differences in past birth rates, the OECD calculates that from 2018 to 2030 Ireland's potential employment growth rate will be 1.2% per annum and France's will be 0.2%.

In contrast, over the same period Germany will experience a potential employment decline of 0.6% per annum, and Finland faces a potential employment decline of 0.2% per year.

These differences partly explain why Germans and Finns see limits to their ability to bail out other countries, like Greece. They know they will soon have fewer people at work, supporting an increasing number of retirees, and they will want to hold their money back for that.

Unfortunately for Greece, it has a similar problem of an ageing and diminishing workforce.

Pensions are already 14.5% of Greece's GDP, compared with 13.8% of France's and almost 11% of Germany's. In contrast, pensions are just a little over 5% of GDP in the UK and Ireland. That difference explains a lot, at least as much as the supposed doctrinal differences between German 'Ordoliberalism' and Anglo–Saxon Keynesianism.

It is true, as Keynesian economists argue, that coordinated demand stimuli, by countries that can afford it, would help Europe's economy achieve its jobs potential, without risk of inflation, and that can come from countries whose fiscal positions are strong. However, the judgement as to which European country can do that has to take account of differences in the ageing profile of each country. Finns and Germans may have the fiscal capacity to stimulate the European economy, but it may be imprudent for them to do so just now because their societies are ageing more rapidly than others.

Incidentally these differences also illustrate the foolishness of anti-immigrant sentiment in Germany. Germany's 6.6 million immigrants paid in €22 billion more in taxes and contributions than they took out in benefits, and some of that surplus is helping pay the pensions of native-born Germans. I expect the same may apply in France.

In fact, the EU Ageing Report, to which I referred earlier, estimates that fifty-five million immigrants will have to come into the EU by 2060, to make up for the decline in our native-born workforce. That can change, of course.

Meanwhile, Africa's population will have increased by 28% by 2060 and Asia's population will have slightly declined.

Europe's youth problem – a wasted generation?
In the next fifty years, on unchanged present trends, the overall working-age population of Europe will drop considerably, from last year's peak of about 300 million to 265 million. This will be a significant blow to nearly every aspect of the Eurozone economy.

At the same time, the old-age dependency ratio – a fraction or percentage expressing the ratio of residents over the age of sixty-five to those under that age – will rise from 28% (recorded earlier this decade) to a staggering 58% by 2060.

The causes of this challenge in Europe are manifold: declining fertility, advances in old-age care, the residue of baby-boom demographics. But the impact will be serious.

The impact is accentuated by the fact that so many of today's youth in Europe are unemployed. The longer they are unemployed, the less relevant their skills become and the harder it will be for them to ever get a well-paid job. Their lifetime earning potential is being radically diminished.

That is a huge medium-term problem that Mario Draghi, President of the European Central Bank, has recognised as the central European problem of today. He said in his speech at Jackson Hole, USA, in 2014, 'The stakes for our monetary union are high. Without permanent cross-country transfers [which he does not expect will happen], a high level of employment in all countries is essential to the long-term cohesion of the euro.'

I would emphasise two words in that sentence: *All* countries in the Eurozone must have a high level of employment. This, according to Draghi, is *essential* for the euro.

Not the sort of language you would expect from a central banker on the subject of employment, which shows that solving Europe's unemployment problem is essential to the survival of the euro, and thus the avoidance of immense financial instability and wealth destruction that would flow from a breakup of the Eurozone.

Even economists like Martin Wolf, who opposed the creation of the euro, argue that its breakup would be an unmitigated disaster at this stage. The breakup of the Eurozone could herald an era, between the countries now in the EU, of arbitrary savings destruction, of national protectionism, of competitive devaluation, and of mutual litigation and recrimination, that would destroy the interdependence that has allowed the European Union itself to be a structure of peace in Europe for sixty years.

Get rid of the euro and we would not be going back to the Europe of the 1980s. We would be going back to the Europe of the 1930s.

And do not forget this: Mario Draghi has linked finding a

solution to high unemployment to avoiding the breakup of the euro.

That is what is at stake.

Today's preschool children will have a heavy economic burden to bear
We will soon not have enough young people in Europe.

From 2030 Europe's working-age population will decline and the number of retired people depending on them will increase. There are four Europeans of working age today for every one retired person. By 2060, there will be only two.

Europe's labour supply will remain stable up to around 2023, and decline thereafter by about nineteen million people by 2060.

As a result of these trends, Europe's relatively small number of pre-school and primary school children of today, will, later in their lives, have to support a proportionately much larger retired population than will their competitors in India, China, and Indonesia. They will also have to support a larger retired population than Europe's workers do today.

Europe will be like a horse carrying extra weight in the 'global competitiveness horse race' of the mid-twenty-first century.

If young people are to have the future earning capacity to bear these extra burdens, it is essential that they get every developmental educational advantage now, no matter what the present income status of their family.

That is not just a matter of social justice – although it certainly is that – it is a matter of pragmatic self-interest for today's, eventually to be retired, workforce and electorate.

But what sort of educational investment will make a difference?

Increasing the teacher/pupil ratio may help, but the evidence on that is ambiguous. Some countries with high teacher ratios perform less well than others who have proportionately fewer teachers.

In fact, it may be before children go to school at all that the biggest improvements in intellectual ability can be achieved.

Children need extra support from the earliest age
A recent report prepared for Vietnam by the World Bank on how that country could improve its educational performance said bluntly: 'Much of the inequality in learning outcomes, between different types of young Vietnamese observed in primary education and beyond, is already established before the age of formal schooling.'

This may be caused by physical poverty, including bad or insufficient nutrition, which will stunt a baby's mental development. Similar poor nutrition will be found in a minority of homes in rich countries too.

But things, like that, that can be explained by lack of money, are not the only factors affecting a child's mental development.

The World Bank Report goes on: 'The brain development of young children is highly sensitive to stimulation and interaction. The more that parents and care givers interact with a young child, for example through talking, singing or reading, the better are the conditions for brain development.'

The report suggests that in Vietnam, babies from better-off families have more of this sort of stimulative interaction with parents and caregivers than do babies in poorer families.

But the general point about what makes a difference applies at all income levels, and if very young children, as they develop, only see their parents for an hour or so each day, and spend the rest of the time away from them, they may lose out on mental development, no matter how well off they may be materially.

If these World Bank views about intellectual development are true, they deserve an urgent response from parents, crèches, and governments at all levels here in Europe.

Research in the United States bears this out. It shows that children who have parents who read to them and answer their questions orally can, by two years of age, have a vocabulary that is four times as great as children who have not had that stimulation. This head start makes a huge difference to their subsequent school career.

The Early Learning Initiative, supported by the National College of Ireland, is addressing this problem in a number of inner-city parishes in Dublin. It provides a system for training local people to become home visitors to families with very small children (0 to 3 years of age) to provide parents with help and encouragement to stimulate their children mentally, to read to them, and help them develop their vocabulary. This initiative has had a dramatic effect in making the children from these parishes 'school ready' at the age of four, when they go to school. Hitherto, many children from the area fell behind at school immediately, never caught up, and dropped out later without any qualification.

If we are going to depend on a smaller number of children to support our welfare systems over the next forty years, we must do everything we can now to enhance their earning capacity, especially by ensuring that they have a happy and stimulating childhood from the earliest age.

That may be the most important long-term economic stimulus of all.

Based on a speech at the dinner of the Institute of Chartered Accountants in Ireland in the Convention Centre, Dublin in January 2015.

WHO BENEFITS FROM GOVERNMENT SOCIAL SPENDING?

There is an ongoing debate about budget cutting in the world today, because revenue is not matching the promise governments made to their people regarding the availability of pensions, unemployment support, and health services.

This problem is particularly acute in countries whose populations are getting older faster, like Finland and Germany.

Who would suffer most if crude across-the-board cuts in government social spending were made? You will find that it would not be the same category of people in every country.

In some countries the top fifth of income earners are the biggest beneficiaries of social supports in the form of cash payments from government.

In fact, France, Italy, Austria, Portugal, Ireland and Spain give a higher share of their cash in social supports (pensions, unemployment and disability supports) to the top fifth of their population than to the bottom fifth.

In contrast, Sweden, the UK, Finland, Belgium, and the US give more to the bottom fifth.

The proportionate share of cash benefits paid to households in the lowest income fifth of the population is highest in Norway and Australia, at 40%, compared to around 10% in Mediterranean countries and 5% in Turkey.

The big difference is means-testing. If benefits are means-tested then a higher portion will be granted to the less well off, but the downside of that can be the creation of poverty traps that impose penalties on people who try to improve their lot, because they then lose benefits.

In some countries, social transfers often go to richer households, because these benefit payments are often related to a work-history in the formal sector, often concerning earnings-related pension payments to retired workers paid by the state. Earnings-related social insurance payments also underlie substantial cash transfers to the top income fifth in Austria, France and Luxembourg.

Perhaps the most striking thing about this chart is that the average OECD country distributes almost exactly 20% of cash benefits to both the top and bottom fifth of the income distribution.

Some governments do less 'social spending' in places where the private sector fills in the gap, particularly when it comes to pensions and health insurance.

In the Netherlands, Denmark, the US, and the UK, for example, private pension payments are worth about 5% of GDP each year, while American spending on private health insurance is worth nearly 6% of GDP.

Some countries spend more on those of pension age, others spend more on those of working age

Pensions paid by government are 5.3% of GDP in Ireland and 5.6% of GDP in the UK, but they are 13.8% of GDP in France, 14.8% in Greece and 10.6% in Germany. In contrast, income support by government for those of working age are 8.3% of GDP in Ireland, as against just 4.7% in France, 5.1% in the UK, 3.8% in Germany and a mere 3% in Greece (notwithstanding that country's high unemployment).

In Ireland's case, it is worth noting that 40% of the unemployed who receive income support from the government are long-term unemployed (i.e. more than a year out of work). The OECD has said that their skill levels are inadequate for the modern economy, which is a big long-term concern.

Meanwhile the number claiming various forms of illness benefit in Ireland has increased by 47% in the last fourteen years, from 150,000 to 220,000. This is surprising in light of the improvements in spending on health services in Ireland since 2000. More has been spent on health, yet more people say they cannot work because of ill health.

Health spending as a percentage of GDP is 8.6% in France and 8% in Germany as against 5.8% of GDP in Ireland, which is below the OECD average of 6.2%. But health spending is rising in Ireland, and the National Competitiveness Council says that, since 2001, Ireland has had the fastest rate of inflation in health insurance costs of seventeen Eurozone countries.

Devising a common policy for the eurozone
These contrasts between countries make it harder to devise a common economic policy, even for the countries who share the euro as their currency. This is ignored by economists who call for a single macroeconomic policy for the Eurozone.

These differences lie behind some of the arguments about immigration in the European Union and the accusations of 'welfare tourism'. These accusations are mostly wrong. In countries where government spending goes to the well-off, one can expect well-placed interest groups to be particularly effective in resisting changes or reductions in expenditure.

Another conflict of interest will be between households with high debts, who are finding it hard to meet their obligations, and households who have made significant savings over the years and who wish to protect the value of those savings.

Household debt, as a percentage of household disposable income, is 326% in Denmark, 288% in the Netherlands and 230% in Ireland, as against 58% in Poland, 90% in Austria and 94% in Germany.

For example, a policy that favoured low interest rates and inflation would benefit the debtors, but hurt the savers. The savers would also have an interest in protecting the value of the bonds issued by banks, companies and governments in which their pension and insurance funds are invested. Debtors, on the other hand, would be more relaxed about 'burning' these bondholders.

These genuine differences of interest need to be brought out into the open; there are reasonable concerns on both sides of the argument and they should be understood by economists, who sometimes simplistically assume one could easily devise a common macroeconomic policy for the Eurozone. There probably is no alternative to the gradual piecemeal process of reform now under way. Different economic habits, built up over the past sixty years, cannot be harmonised quickly.

THE CHALLENGES FACING ECONOMICS IN IRELAND

The recent economic crisis has been good for economists (they are in demand as members of panels of all kinds, so as to explain what went wrong) but it has not been so good for the science of economics, in the sense that so few people with economic training foresaw either the scale, or the timing, of the collapse.

Why did the science of economics not foresee the crisis and offer preventative suggestions?
It is possible to argue that foreseeing the timing of the collapse was a lot to ask. Sometimes a random event can occur, which will set off a chain of events that will topple an economic set up that was already unstable, and it is difficult to know which random event will be the one to have that effect, or to predict when it will happen. Obviously the sooner it happens the better, because a lesser adjustment will then be necessary.

Less easy to understand is why the bulk of the economic profession worldwide did not grasp the fact that the scale of the imbalances in the world had grown so great, that the gradual 'soft landing' that most seemed to have assumed would happen was inherently unlikely. Virtually all the major international bodies expected a soft landing.

Given that everyone knew that paper money itself is based purely on confidence and trust (the paper itself is worth nothing), and that most money in use is actually bank credit, while most banks cannot resist a sustained bank run, it is hard to see how so many economists could have assumed that unsustainable positions could be unwound slowly, over a long period, without somebody panicking at some stage – thereby precipitating a bank run.

Yet, that seems to have been the general assumption.

Why were balance of payments and house price data ignored?
In Ireland's case, there was published data which showed clearly that, although we were part of a single currency that we had no power to devalue, we were running a large balance of payments deficit. In other words we were spending more abroad than we were earning. Ireland had a very large balance of payments deficit in 2005 (€5,690 million) and had been running a deficit in every year since 2000. Meanwhile, new house prices had risen by 64% since 2000, whereas consumer prices (excluding mortgages) had only risen by 18%. These figures were known at the time. Economists and others believed, mistakenly, that the balance of payments did not matter in a currency union, and the potential danger of private sector imbalances was ignored.

Some Irish economists, and non-economists, may have sensed that there was something radically wrong here, but the consensus remained that the position would unwind slowly and relatively painlessly.

But *how* was it supposed to unwind?

How were exports supposed to accelerate and catch up with imports, which was the only way the balance of payments could correct itself without a domestic recession being used to curb imports?

How were incomes of households in Ireland supposed to catch up with house prices, without a fall in house prices which would undermine the basis on which people were contracting mortgages, and without thereby creating a banking crisis?

What economic strategy or projection was there for such a major increase in incomes in Ireland? What economic strategy was there for an increase in exports sufficient to overtake imports and eliminate the balance of payments gap? Given that we were buying the imports on credit, surely this raised questions about our banking system?

I have no doubt that some economists were asking these

questions, but they were not being heard.
Why was this?

Busy optimists had neither the time nor inclination to heed the warning signs
One reason is that people did not take the time to listen. They were too busy – busy making money, meeting their quarterly targets, winning votes, or doing all the other things that make up a modern, crowded life. Most people did not have – or did not make – the time to think things out.

Furthermore, I believe any economist who sounded a warning was not being heard because of a good trait of human nature which serves us well in normal times – optimism. If humans were not optimists, they would not have taken the risks which, after much trial and error, brought about advances in technology from the earliest times, from the domestication of wild animals to the invention of the Internet.

But lack of time, and optimism, were also present in other countries which did not have property bubbles, countries like Canada and Germany.

There may thus be other factors to look at, principally the recent economic history of Ireland.

Blinded by recent success, the source of which was not fully understood
In Ireland's case, we had, from 1994 to 2000, a surge in economic growth, which was based on solid technological advances and improved cost competitiveness and productivity.

This surge was the result of improvements that had been made long before, but at the time that was not widely understood and we thus drew the wrong conclusions from our growth performance in the 1994 to 2000 period. This growth was, in good measure, a one-off harvesting of the fruits of previous investment, a harvest that had been artificially delayed by extraneous events.

Ireland had been held back relative to the rest of Europe in the post-war decades by poor education, by protectionism, by over dependence on one market and a few products, and by a neglect of technology. Up to 1970, we were a long distance from the 'productivity frontier', such as the levels of productivity being achieved in the United States.

In the 1966 to 1973 period these defects were put right. And in a sense, the Celtic Tiger should have happened in the mid-1970s, rather than in the mid-1990s. Remember, there was a big return of emigrants to Ireland in the 1970s, many of whom were children, which was a good sign for the future. But the Celtic Tiger was postponed by external developments. In 1974, we were hit by the oil crisis, which dramatically worsened our balance of payments and public finances.

In the 1980s, we were hit by the huge hike in interest rates, initiated by Paul Volcker of the Federal Reserve, to squeeze inflation out of the system. This rise in interest rates caused a crisis in the public finances of Ireland in 1981, because we had exposed ourselves as a result of unwise government borrowing in the late 1970s.

Then, in the early 1990s, when we should have been recovering quickly, we were hit by renewed higher interest rates. This arose from currency exchange rate instability in Europe.

There was another factor at work: demography. Ireland's birth rate had been very high in the 1970s and peaked in 1980. So we had a disproportionately large number of children in the country in the 1980s. These children were too young to earn anything and had to be provided for by a relatively small working population.

By the mid-1990s, some of these young people were entering the workforce, and furthermore women were taking up paid work much more than before. The combination of these two changes resulted in the workforce in 1990s Ireland being almost twice what it had been in the 1980s.

The growth rates of the 1994–2000 period were a one-off
Once external constraints, like artificially high oil prices and interest rates, were removed, and the working population increased, all was set for a surge forward in economic activity. But this also meant that we came much closer to the global 'productivity frontier', beyond which further advance is only possible through profound technological advances.

Looking at how we responded to the crisis, in the period from 2008 to date, it is important to stress that the fundamental structural advantages of the Irish economy – the base of high-tech industry and services, and the flexibility of our workforce – were preserved.

Indeed, competitiveness was improved quickly, and the success in negotiating pay reductions and economies in the public sector was remarkable. Some progress was made in reducing private debt, which had reached around 220% of gross disposable income in 2010.

On the other hand, government debt rose from 40% of GDP in 2008 to 124% today. While some of this was due to the cost of recapitalising banks, the bulk of the increase in debt was due to borrowing to bridge the gap that had suddenly grown between previously inflated spending levels and presently depleted revenues.

Escaping the debt trap:
when nominal growth rates exceed the rate of interest
Responsible finance is neither a left-wing nor a right-wing idea. It is common sense.

To escape from the debt situation we are in, we need to reach a point where our nominal GDP is rising faster than the rate of interest we are paying. The Department of Finance says that our nominal GDP growth rate this year (2014) is 2.8%, whereas our interest rate is 4%, and our deficit to be met by government borrowing is to be 4.8% of GDP. But by 2018, they expect our nominal GDP growth rate will be 5.4%, as against an interest rate of 4.4%, and that we will have a budget surplus of 0.5% of GDP. Thus, we should, in 2018, be in a position where our debt/GDP ratio will be falling, rather than rising.

Obviously, if the department has overestimated our likely nominal growth rate, or if we fail to meet the targets for reduced borrowing, that happy outcome will not happen. We are not in complete control of any of these variables.

The one we have most control over is our gap between spending and revenue, but even that can be affected by international trade and interest rate conditions, which can increase spending or reduce revenues.

Interest rates could be raised above the expected level, as they were in the early 1980s, if either central bankers start worrying about rising inflationary expectations, or if lenders are hit by a sovereign default somewhere else, either in the Eurozone or otherwise. This could become a problem when we have to roll over existing fixed-rate borrowings. Conversely, if deflation sets in, the real value of our debts would start to rise, despite not increasing them in nominal terms.

Nominal growth can be raised in two ways: by inflation or by real increases in output. Inflation, which would also reduce the real value of our debts, seems unlikely. So we will have to rely on real output increases, which we can either sell abroad as exports or sell to ourselves.

Some see a boost to domestic demand as part of the solution, but that would be counterproductive if it meant that we stopped reducing our very high household debts, or increased salaries and wages in a way that diminished our ability to compete on export markets. We rely on export performance to bring in the money that will enable us to get our debts under control. Much of any stimulus to domestic demand would seep away into imports very quickly. We would be stimulating someone else's economy.

In the longer term, we are also bound by a treaty, approved in a referendum by the Irish people, to reduce our debt/GDP ratio at a steady pace, down to 60% of GDP, from its present level of 124%.

Committed by treaty to having budget surpluses, while also coping with upward spending pressures
This will mean running primary budget surpluses year after year. A primary surplus is a surplus of revenue over all expenditure, except debt service. This will not be an easy sell in an ageing society, where demands for more spending, especially on health, will be very strong.

It is important to reflect on the present inbuilt tendency of government spending to rise, even when no policy decision to raise it is taken.

As Brendan Howlin, Minister for Public Expenditure and Reform, pointed out in his budget speech, with no policy change since 2008, the number of people of pensionable age increased by 13.5%, the number of medical card holders by 40%, and the numbers in schools and universities by 8%.

This year alone, social welfare pension costs will increase by €190 million and public service pension costs by €77 million. Meanwhile next year, some of the Haddington Road pay savings will expire when the Haddington Road Agreement (the outcome of negotiations between public service management and unions, which took place in May 2013) itself expires.

So even if there are no tax cuts and no new spending ideas, keeping spending down to the level required to meet the deficit targets will be hard work.

Indeed it will be important that election manifestos are compatible with the treaty obligations we have undertaken. One suggestion is that election manifestos should be costed in advance by the Fiscal Advisory Council.

It is in Ireland's interest to ensure all eurozone states respect the treaty
Matching the pressures of national politics with mutual treaty obligations to control debt for the sake of our shared currency will be a challenge for every democracy in the Eurozone, including in countries like Germany, France and Italy, which have a lower long-term growth potential than we do.

Indeed it will be in our interest that others are seen to respect their treaty obligations too, because doubts about the viability of sovereign borrowing in any Eurozone country could have an immediate knock-on effect on the interest we would pay on our sovereign borrowing, and that could throw our plans off course.

Our future is, of course, inextricably linked up with the future of the euro, and thus of the European Union. Worries about the future of the euro have diminished, but have not disappeared.

The fragility of the EU lies in the extent to which power has gravitated back to the big member states at the expense of the common EU interest, as expressed through the Commission, Council of Ministers, and Parliament. New items have since come on to the agenda, and inadequate provisions have been made for these in existing treaties. Power has been renationalised, and that suits big states, not small ones.

Ireland's rejection of previous EU treaties has, entirely unintentionally and indirectly, contributed to this process by making EU leaders reluctant to propose treaty amendments that might restore more initiative to the traditional EU decision-making process, which works better for small countries.

The need for integrated democracy in Europe
Economists understand the power of incentives.

In the European Council, where the real power now lies, no member has a strong political incentive to put the collective interests of Europe before the interests of his/her own country.

Even the Commission, because of its method of appointment, has an incentive to consult the interests of the big states first.

That is why I believe, if the EU is to succeed, it needs some form of supranational democracy that will create a political mandate, derived from all the people of Europe, that will be large enough to take precedence over even the biggest state. Improving scrutiny of EU policies in twenty-eight national parliaments is not enough.

I believe that either the President of the Commission, or the President of the European Council, should be directly elected by the people of Europe.

Unless something radical like that is done, I fear that the EU and the euro will continue to be blamed for the consequences of failures of national policies, failures that will have only a slight connection with the euro. If that happens, the permissive consent of citizens, which allows the EU to exist and grow, will disappear.

That would be an economic and political disaster, for the EU and its neighbours, far greater than the crash of 2008.

Undue increases in the gap between winners and losers can undermine the system
The issue of growing inequality in some western economies is different from the issue of whether or not we should live within

our means. Yet they are often confused in public debate by people who want to be popular, and dodge the true implications of what they are demanding.

We need to look at the factors that are driving inequality, because if the outcomes of economic policy create unduly wide divergences between winners and losers, the whole system will be undermined.

Taxation is one factor that can aggravate inequality, but in Ireland we already have a relatively progressive tax system. We are also beginning to tax property, which is only fair. However, we have to remember that people can move residence to avoid unduly progressive taxes. Some high earners coming here from abroad bring jobs for others into the country, and we would like them to stay here.

It is arguable that quantitative easing, by boosting share prices, has added to inequality, because only the better off tend to have a lot of shares and financial instruments, and are thus in a position to benefit from the increase in their nominal value.

It is also arguable that systems of executive compensation, which reward short-term gains in share prices, encourage business managements to favour the buying back of shares over investment, add to inequality, and depress long-term growth. Pay systems that reward short-term results are particularly noxious in the financial sector.

The celebrity factor has also added to income inequality, because all sorts of businesses, like football clubs, recognise the importance of holding on to the celebrity managers or players, as a means of boosting stock prices, match attendances, or TV revenues.

Given that we live in a globalised world, it is difficult for one country to deal with these issues on its own without provoking a flight of capital and talent to other countries. Imagine what would happen to the success rate of football clubs in a country that decided unilaterally to cap the pay rates of players in the interests of equality!

People with rare skills, that command disproportionate rewards, and thus make for more inequality in incomes, can move more and more easily from country to country. If any one country wants to attract those skills, it has to make it attractive for people to live and work in their country.

To address some of the causes of the growth of inequality, international understandings will be necessary. The OECD and the EU are the venues in which some of the causes can be tackled, but it will not be easy.

Structuring the economy to promote growth
I will turn, finally, to the things we might do to boost economic growth. This is not an area in which economists have reached a final consensus.

The prevailing view is that the best way to promote growth is to encourage labour and capital to move freely from one activity to another, so as to find the activities with the highest rate of return. High legal costs, restrictions on entry to professions, state monopolies of particular activities, and big barriers to redundancy of workers, all work against freedom to allocate resources efficiently, and thereby inhibit growth. In Ireland's case we still have high legal costs, and a problem of monopoly pricing in the energy sector.

But it is also possible that markets can be *too* efficient, at least in a short-term sense. For example, banks were too efficient in lending money here during the boom.

Returns to pension funds have declined, notwithstanding the additional sophistication of the independent fund managers. UK pension funds earned a 5% return on capital between 1963 and 1999. But between 2000 and 2009, they earned only 1.1% return. That's not financially sustainable. Why did this happen? Low interest rates promoted by central banks are part of the problem.

Incentives to unduly rapid turnover of investments are also blamed by some.

To remedy this, suggestions for reform of the incentive structure of fund managers have been made. Worries have been expressed about bonuses earned from artificially rapid turnover in shares held on behalf of pension funds, and about 'momentum trading', where an attempt is made to make gains by anticipating the momentum of the market, rather than by focusing on underlying returns.

I do not feel able to judge these matters, or to say what, if anything, we should do about them in this jurisdiction. However, the fundamental point I would make is that capitalism works best when it is subject to good, clear and simple rules, which strike the right balance between promoting lively competition in the here and now, and taking a long-term view of investments that will yield the best returns over time.

The international financial service sector is part of Ireland's export success story. Exports of services now make up 52% of all Irish exports, with financial services, software and business services making up the bulk of this. The opportunities are enormous.

The global middle class, the class that saves for a private pension, is set to treble by 2040. This is a major market opportunity for the Irish funds industry.

The urban population of the world is set to increase by 75% by 2050. This will require huge infrastructural investment in roads, water treatment, electricity, and other forms of infrastructure. As a centre of excellence in both finance, and sustainable technology, this is also an opportunity for Ireland, and particularly for the Green IFSC.

The international financial services industry needs to make a big investment in information technology and social media. For example, Ireland is gaining a leading position in information technology through the design, by Intel in Ireland, of the Quark X1000 chip.

If a country is able to host the designers of big technological breakthroughs like this, it is breaking through the 'productivity frontier', to which I referred earlier. Again, this is an opportunity for Ireland to connect its financial service expertise with its information technology expertise, and its hosting of firms like Google, Facebook, and Paypal.

This is, I believe, the key to promoting economic growth – making new connections. Economic growth is about a state of mind, in individuals and in society. About failing and still trying again.

Based on the Keynote Speech at the Trinity Economics Forum, in the Long Room Hub, Trinity College, Dublin in February 2014.

Environment

HOW CAN WE ACHIEVE A LONG-TERM, SUSTAINABLE ENERGY SUPPLY FOR THE WORLD

⁂

We will, sometime or other, possibly when most of those alive today have departed, run out of oil, gas and coal. While it is the case that known reserves of fossil fuel are increasing, not reducing, thanks to new technologies (like shale gas and horizontal drilling), the reality remains that fossil fuels are inherently finite. They will run out. We do not know when but run out they will, eventually.

Gulf states, like the United Arab Emirates, Saudi Arabia, and Kuwait have substantial renewable energy potential, especially for the use of solar panels, whenever solar energy becomes competitive in price with coal, oil and gas. This will happen, but there is a lot more research and development to be done first.

Renewable energies do not yet compete on price, but subsidies are justified
One estimate of the present price of electricity from different sources suggested that:

- Natural gas and coal could produce electricity at around €70 per megawatt hour,
- Onshore wind could produce it at €135 per megawatt hour,
- Offshore wind could produce it at €220 per megawatt hour and
- Rooftop solar could produce it at €325 per megawatt hour.

This is why, for the time being, renewable energy needs some form of subsidy if it is to be put into operation, so that technical problems, that are likely to arise with any new technology, are identified and resolved in time. Only thus will the renewable technologies be made workable at a reasonable cost in sufficient time to replace fossil fuels.

This subsidy is economically justified for two reasons:

1. Oil, gas, and coal will eventually run out, and we need ready alternatives that have been road tested and ready for use as a replacement
2. The normal supply price of coal and gas does not include any sum to cover the long-term financial damage caused by the climate change generated by coal and gas burning, and if we are to avoid a climate shock we need to gradually reduce consumption of fossil fuels by making it more costly than renewable energy sources.

CO_2 emissions are speeding up, not slowing down
Climate change caused by the burning of fossil fuels is a huge problem. The substitution of natural gas for coal will slow it down, because it generates less CO_2, but it will not reverse the progressive increase of the amount of CO_2 in the atmosphere. This has grown from 355ppm in 1990, to 370ppm in 2000, to 390ppm today.

Despite all the summit conferences, the rate at which CO_2 is being emitted is now speeding up, not slowing down. We can see the results in the melting of the Arctic ice cap and the worrying and unpredictable effects it is having on our weather.

Renewable energy production will increase too slowly to stop climate change
Renewable fuels will not, unless the price at which they are available is dramatically reduced, provide an answer to this problem. This is because long-term global demand for energy is growing so fast – far faster than our renewable energy supply.

Even assuming a carbon price of €70 per tonne (hoped to be put in place by governments to disincentivise fossil fuel use), one estimate suggested that:

- Wind power use in electricity will increase sevenfold by 2040, from just 2% of global energy production today to 7% by 2040, because demand will have increased so much.
- Solar power use will increase twentyfold, but will still only provide 2% of global electricity by 2040, again because it will not increase fast enough to keep up with the rapid growth in electricity demand.

Today we are politically a long way from putting a global €70 per tonne price on carbon, which is what would be necessary to force a general switch to renewables. The United States, with its newly discovered resources of oil and gas, would resist this bitterly.

In most countries, including the United States, there is no charge levied for pumping CO_2 into the atmosphere.

In some countries, including some Arab countries and countries that will ultimately suffer most from climate change, the production and use of fossil fuels is actually being subsidised. In other words, those countries are subsidising global warming, even though their people will suffer more than most from it. Taking such subsidies away would be very unpopular in those countries.

In the EU, where there is a charge for a permit under the Emission Trading Scheme, it is only at €7 per tonne at the moment, because when the scheme was being introduced governments insisted on issuing so many free permits to their heavy industries. It is far below the price needed to encourage large-scale substitution of renewable energy for fossil fuels.

Electricity will be the big culprit
The biggest increase in CO_2 emissions in the future will come from electricity generation. Global electricity demand will grow by 85% by 2040. Heavy industry will be a big user, but so too will the information technology sector. Digital warehouses already use the equivalent of the electricity that would be generated by thirty nuclear power stations.

And the decision by countries, like Germany, to abandon nuclear power will increase their use of coal to generate electricity.

I believe this decision, driven by electoral considerations in the wake of the Fukushima nuclear plant accident in Japan, was a mistake. The evidence suggests that the negative impact on human health from coal burning has been cumulatively much greater than anything attributable to nuclear power generation. But nuclear accidents create drama, whereas the health damage caused by coal burning is a daily phenomenon, which does not make for a big news story.

The most rapid increase of all in coal-fired electricity generation is taking place in China, although China is also leading the world in renewable energy development. Coal-fired plants emit thirty-two times as much CO_2 as gas-fired plants.

Long-term project finance is needed
The tightening up of credit following the financial crisis has also made it more difficult to deal with the impending climate crisis. The funds are not available to finance the big structural changes that are necessary. Quantitative easing has increased the availability of funds, but this has not led to major investment in renewables. This may be due to the temporary fall in oil prices and to general uncertainty. Governments who would in the past have led the way in such investments are focusing on reducing their debts and deficits.

Substituting renewable energy for fossil fuels, and improving energy efficiency by recycling lighter materials will require large capital investment. The new Basel III rules for banks – a global, voluntary regulatory framework on bank capital adequacy, stress testing and market liquidity risk – will make it impossible, or at least very difficult, for banks to be funders or investors in long-term infrastructure projects.

Pension funds could be a source of long-term funding for renewable infrastructure, but they have little expertise in the field.

This is a market that Ireland, with its established expertise in the international asset management and funds industries, is seeking to serve through the Green IFSC. Finding a way to provide long-term finance for renewable energy, and enhancing its efficiency should be top priorities of the EU.

A long-term solution: putting a realistic price on climate damage
The response to the financial crisis has reminded us that knowing we have a problem, and doing something about it, are two very different things.

The problem of a huge buildup of credit in some Eurozone countries, and consequent huge payment imbalances, was known to EU policymakers as early as 2003, but nothing was done about it until recently.

A financial and banking crisis was first needed to create enough anxiety among the public to give policymakers impetus to take action.

It took the collapse of Lehman Brothers, and a stall in Europe's banking system, to generate a willingness to do something about the underlying economic and fiscal imbalances in the developed world.

Notwithstanding the level of unemployment in the developed world, the EU still taxes labour more heavily than it does carbon emissions. A global shift away from taxation of labour to taxation of finite resource use, on the scale necessary to make a difference, would be politically very difficult because it would redistribute prosperity in favour of those of working age, to the detriment of others.

In short, it would mean pensioners would be paying a lot more for their coal and electricity, while employees paid a lot less income tax and social security contributions. The political consequences of such a shift would be dramatic.

It would require a major crisis, which could be clearly shown to have been caused by climate change, to make this politically feasible. Perhaps major flooding in low-lying, highly-populated areas along the coasts of Europe might be the kickstarter. But even if that were to happen, it could already be too late.

Such a crisis might make it politically possible to consider radical solutions, such as a high carbon tax, with an accompanying levy or tariff on the carbon content of imports. A high carbon tax in one country, without some levy on imports, would simply penalise industry in that country. Such a proposal would get no support at the moment. But its time may come.

Dramatic increases in carbon taxes may prove so difficult that it may seem easier to simply ban particularly damaging activities, such as the operation of coal-fired power stations. That might be politically feasible in countries that do not have a lot of coal, but not so easy in countries like Poland, who have a lot of coal and would subsequently be forced to rely on Russian gas if they could not use their own coal.

In any serious attempt to deal with climate change there will be winners and losers. A mechanism must be devised for the winners to compensate the losers. That can be done within a country that has a single tax system, but it is much more difficult to do between countries, as climate change negotiators have found.

The above material was first presented at the Dubai Energy Forum in April 2013.

THE POLITICAL CONSEQUENCES OF WASTE

From 2011 to 2014, I was chairman of the European Sustainable Materials Platform.

The platform brought together European commissioners, MEPs, government ministers, NGOs and business representatives. The aim was to agree a strategy on how to reduce Europe's use of any finite material resources.

Unfortunately the platform was abolished by the Juncker Commission, under pressure from those who want the European Commission to do less and leave more to the member states. I think this was a mistake because the waste of scarce, irreplaceable materials is not something that can be stopped at the level of individual states; it needs a European and a global solution, and the platform was taking the first tentative steps towards finding such a solution on a European basis.

In the course of their daily lives, Europeans use up fifteen tonnes of physical material every year. 80% of it is never recycled. Much of the waste is derived from a non-renewable resource dug up from the ground.

Some of the waste we throw away contains materials whose scarcity could be used in the future as a form of political blackmail by those who control supply. A third of the fifteen tonnes of material each European uses up every year is imported from outside the EU, much of it from politically unstable places like Russia and the Middle East. The wasteful use of resources creates strategic vulnerability.

The oil crisis of the 1970s was a notable example of the use of the scarcity of a finite material to achieve a political goal. The present dependency of EU countries on Russian natural gas is another example. If Russia supplies 40% of Europe's gas, that reduces Europe's political independence of Russia.

Energy is not the only area in which Europe needs a common policy if it is to maintain its political independence and freedom of action. A little-discussed but very important example of a finite resource which could be used for blackmail is phosphate.

It is anticipated by some that the world's known phosphate deposits could be exhausted by the end of the century. The largest phosphate deposits are found in Morocco, the United States, and China. Although phosphorus is used for other purposes, its use in agricultural fertilisers is critical for the future of civilisation. Heavy users of phosphate, like Ireland and the rest of Europe, have no indigenous supplies. We need to ask ourselves what would happen if, for any reason, Morocco, the United States or China decided that they would cease exporting phosphate to us. Likewise, we need to ask what will happen when phosphate runs out.

Without mineral phosphate, I doubt if the world's agricultural land could feed the world's present population.

While renewable energy sources are a substitute (albeit an expensive one) for fossil fuels, there is no known substitute for phosphate used in agriculture. It may be a sign of things to come but phosphate prices have trebled since 2000. Today much of the fertiliser phosphate that is used is being wasted, washed away into streams and rivers. Excessive run-off of this mineral induces algal blooms in lakes and rivers and contributes to ocean dead zones.

Other non-renewable resources modern societies depend upon include:

- Zinc,
- Iron ore,
- Bauxite (to make aluminium), and
- 'Rare earths' (used in many electronic gadgets including smart phones, most of which are never recycled).

Water is another scarce resource that needs to be used sparingly. Some forms of irrigated agricultural production, particularly in hot countries, are running down irreplaceable supplies of underground water resources that are not being naturally replenished.

Some of the food produced by the usage of that irreplaceable water is then being flown to far away markets, using untaxed aircraft fuel that is also derived from finite, irreplaceable oil supplies.

Now is the time for Europeans to start economising on our use of non-renewable resources for the sake of our lives, and of our political independence. Europe must find a way to decouple economic growth from the depletion of all resources that will eventually run out.

- We must increase our productivity by getting more income from less physical material. We must measure and improve the material resource productivity of our economy, just as we measure and seek to improve the labour productivity of our economy.
- We must reuse material, rather than dump it.
- We must insulate our dwellings properly.
- We must replace non-renewable energy supplies with renewable ones. This will involve reorganising our electricity grid, which in turn will also involve pylons and wind turbines (to which some mistakenly object).

The era of very cheap air travel may end if, in the interests of fair competition, airline fuel were to be taxed on the same basis as fuel used in road transport. That would be particularly severe for islands like Ireland which depend on air travel more than continental countries.

In the short run, all this will be costly and politically difficult, and households, businesses and countries may need to be given financial incentives that mitigate those costs.

Getting twenty-eight countries in the European Union to agree on issues like this will be far from easy, but it is ultimately a matter of political survival.

It is better to do something now, and do it gradually, than to wait for a war, or some other crisis, to force us to do it all suddenly.

URBANISATION
– AN INEXORABLE TREND, BUT IS IT GOOD FOR US?

In global terms, the pull of ever bigger cities seems inexorable.

In 1970, a third of the world's population lived in cities, more than half do so today, and it is predicted that by 2050 two-thirds of the world's nine billion people will live in cities.

City dwellers consume more energy per capita, produce more greenhouse gases per capita, and are more exposed to crime. A 1% increase in the urban population leads to a 2.5% increase in energy use. Cities often expand close to the coastline, where they will be proportionately more exposed to rising sea levels caused by climate change.

Big cities lead to anonymous, atomised lives for many; people become lost in the crowd. This makes big cities harder to govern democratically, because the social networks that may facilitate democracy, discussion and consensus in rural areas, are often missing in big cities.

Yet people seem to prefer to live in cities. Why?

A recent study says that, on average, the bigger the city, the bigger the income per person, and the higher the proportion of the population with higher-level degrees. But the same study also shows that the bigger the city, the higher is the incidence of anxiety and transmissible diseases.

A study published by the Royal Society in London, using data collected from tracking people and their mobile phones, suggests that the bigger the city the more friends people have, but also the more frequently they change their friends. It even discovered that the bigger the city, the faster people walk, probably reflecting higher stress levels.

Attaching importance to things that can be measured in money seems to drive this rapid urbanisation of the world's population. But one must stand back and ask if this sort of living is best for children growing up, if it facilitates children having enough time with their parents, and if it is good for the quality and cost of the schooling children receive. One must also ask if rapid urbanisation makes it harder for people to care for elderly relatives or for children to have regular contact with their grandparents – all things that are important to the quality of life. A living pattern that is not good for children may not be sustainable in the long run.

This drive to live in ever bigger cities seems also to be a part of the increased specialisation of people's lives. Jobs have become so technical that fewer people understand the work that their next-door neighbour does, and only in bigger cities will one find a critical mass of people with specific inter-relatable skills. That's what attracts firms to big cities and may explain why property prices in Dublin are more dynamic than elsewhere.

As a small island off another island, distant from the European mainland, Ireland has done exceptionally well to develop critical masses of skilled people in sectors like pharmaceuticals, medical devices, software, certain financial services, use of big data and food technologies.

Foreign direct investment continued to come into this country in these sectors even in the worst period of the recession.

As I worked abroad for IFSC Ireland, I was repeatedly told that what attracts firms here is the ability to recruit the right people, either locally or among people who are willing to come here to live and work.

It is thanks to this continuing overseas confidence in the Irish economy that we have been able to meet our fiscal targets, borrow at reasonable rates, and restore economic growth. But such confidence is volatile and fragile, and prone to sudden changes in sentiment due to media headlines. We must remain vigilant. Since the abolition of exchange controls, money can come into a country quickly. But it can also leave it quickly – money often has the legs of a hare, but the courage of a mouse. That is why confidence must be constantly maintained by steady management and consistent fiscal policy.

History

THE LEGACY OF PARNELL

HOME RULE: THE STEPPING STONE TO INDEPENDENCE,
WITHOUT VIOLENCE

∽

Parnell entered the House of Commons as a member for Meath in 1875 in a by-election. He had previously contested a by-election in County Dublin, but was defeated there by the Conservative candidate Colonel Taylor of Ardgillan, a result which demonstrates the invincibility of the Taylors in every century.

Interestingly, in light of subsequent events, the twenty-seven-year-old Parnell relied heavily, in order to secure the home rule nomination to stand in both contests, on a fulsome endorsement from his local Catholic parish priest, Fr Richard Galvin of Rathdrum.

Fr Galvin described Parnell as 'up to the mark' on all the great questions of the day, which for him meant home rule, denominational education and fixity of tenure.

After losing in Dublin, in seeking the nomination in Meath, Parnell had an animated interview with the Catholic Bishop of Meath, Thomas Nulty. He secured the bishop's support, and the highlight of his successful campaign, according to his biographer, F. S. L. Lyons, was a great meeting in Navan, attended, *inter alia*, by many parish priests and curates.

Religious belief, ethics, and education
In the campaign, Parnell committed himself to denominational education 'under the proper control of the clergy', as he put it.

Indeed he subsequently supported denominational education at university level too.

The issue of denominational education has been a live issue in Irish politics since the 1830s and remains so to this day. As Parnell recognised, Irish people saw a link between ethical formation and religious belief, and thus favoured denominational involvement in education, as most of them still do. Exactly how this is to be done is a matter of balance, which alters over time. Denominational education preserves diversity, something Parnell wanted in a home rule Ireland.

Facing an economic crisis
Very early in Parnell's parliamentary career, Ireland faced a sudden fall in income, partly due to the forces of globalisation.

The heavy concentration of small holdings on the western seaboard meant that, in this heavily populated part of the country, people had a very precarious livelihood.

In the 1870s, the immensely fertile grain-growing regions of the mid-western United States gained access to the global market, thanks to massive railway construction and improved shipping. These regions were able to supply grains to Europe at prices well below those at which Irish, British, and other European farmers could produce them.

This meant an immediate fall in farm incomes in these islands, and a fall in the demand for migratory seasonal labour in Scotland and the east of Ireland, on which many western farmers had come to depend to supplement their incomes and pay their rent.

And then, in 1879, there was a disastrous summer, and blight again afflicted the potato crop. Potato production plunged from 4 million tons in 1876 to only 1 million in 1879. People began to starve.

Turning a crisis into an opportunity
Parnell saw this crisis as an emergency, but also as an opportunity. He sent some of his lieutenants to the United States to raise funds to relieve starvation in Ireland, *and* to fund a new National Land

League to campaign for a change in the basis of land ownership in Ireland. Through the New Departure, he won Fenian support for this campaign by linking it with the cause of self-government for Ireland.

Parnell's ability to turn what was objectively a humanitarian disaster into a vehicle for political and economic reform, marks him out as a politician of exceptional talent.

The ideas were not all his own, but he could fuse them into something potent. It is fair to say that the disastrous fall in incomes that occurred in the late 1870s would have happened no matter what system of land tenure, or of government, Ireland then had, so it took someone of Parnell's talent to turn it into something more far-reaching.

This is something that current Irish political leaders can draw from Parnell's career in facing today's economic crisis. In a crisis, it is possible to get people to see things differently, and to agree to changes they might not undertake in calmer and less anxious times.

The role of disciplined political parties
Parnell's career also demonstrates the value of grass-roots political organisation, and disciplined parliamentary parties.

The Irish Parliamentary Party, of which Parnell became the first leader in 1884, was the first disciplined parliamentary party of its kind in the House of Commons, and perhaps in the world.

It became the model for others. Members were bound by a pledge, signed before they were accepted as candidates, and agreed to sit, act and vote on the basis of collective majority decisions.

I believe it is part of Parnell's legacy that Irish parliamentary parties in Dáil Éireann, 130 years later, are more disciplined in the way they vote than in equivalent situations in the UK, and indeed in most European countries, and certainly more than in the US.

This is a strength in Irish politics, which can be traced back to Parnell.

While party discipline has downsides, it creates conditions in which decisions, once made, can be quickly and coherently implemented. This is important in dealing with a crisis.

Party discipline in this Dáil was one of the factors which enabled the Irish governments of the day to act more quickly in dealing with financial crises than most other European states were able to do.

Imagine what it would have been like in the last four years if the Dáil consisted of 166 entirely independent members, responsible only to their own particular constituencies, or of members, like in the United States, who were beholden to special interests and could ignore the collective view of their party. A speedy response to the crisis would have been impossible. Where the party pledge proved, unfortunately, to be much less operative was in Parnell's own case.

He did not apply the principle of collective majority decisions to his own position as leader. That position then came into question when in the wake of the revelations in the O'Shea divorce case, Gladstone stated that the Liberal Party's alliance with the Irish Parliamentary Party would cease because of the impact the case had on the opinion of the Liberal grass roots.

Although a clear majority of the Irish Party MPs wanted Parnell to step down, partially or fully, Parnell would not accept the majority verdict, something that would not happen in any Irish parliamentary party today.

Parnell's approach to the land question
Parnell's approach to the land question was more nuanced than one might think. Unlike Michael Davitt and most of his own party, he did not favour what eventually happened – the outright and compulsory transfer from the landlord to the farmer who was already farming the land.

He proposed an amendment in 1888 which would have restricted tenant purchase to holdings where the rateable valuation (PLV) was £20, a small farm of no more than 30 acres. Later he revised the figure up to £50 PLV.

He seems to have wanted to allow the survival of small residential Irish landlords (like himself), and only wanted compulsory transfer of the holdings of the absentee landlords. He argued that residential landlords were 'well fitted' to 'take part in the future social regeneration' of a home rule Ireland. Frank Callanan, historian and author of *The Parnell Split, 1890–91* (Cork University Press, 1992), has speculated that he took this middle course with a view to reducing Protestant landholding opposition to home rule, and perhaps as a bridge to Unionism more generally.

But his party did not support his position. Indeed this may explain why, when the party split over his leadership, Parnell's support was weakest in counties like Carlow, where there was a significant presence of large tenant farmers who aspired to be owner occupiers, and had holdings bigger than Parnell's upper limit of fifty or sixty acres.

A local angle

As previously mentioned, Parnell was first elected to represent Meath. It was my honour to also represent this county ninety years later.

I remember in my first campaign in 1969 meeting a neighbour, Charlie Curley of Castlefarm, who told me his father had been an ardent Parnellite and had heard Parnell speak under the Big Tree in Dunboyne village. The tree still stands, a mute memorial to the deceased leader.

Dunboyne was a Parnellite parish, but during the split, the local parish priest preached a particularly strong sermon against Parnell. A majority of local people decided to punish the parish priest by not making offerings at funerals. As a result, until funeral offerings were finally ended in the 1970s in Meath, Dunboyne was the only parish in which they did not take place.

The Parnell split in Meath is well described in *Divine Right? The Parnell Split in Meath* (Cork University Press, 2007), an excellent book by David Lawlor, whose own grandfather was involved.

Reading his book, I was amazed to discover how many of the descendants of the protagonists in the split were still active in local politics. One was the long-time chairman of Meath County Council, and political ally of my own, the late Paddy Fullam, whose grandfather had been elected as an anti-Parnellite MP in South Meath, only to be unseated as a result of a Parnellite election petition.

A CENTENARY OF A VICTORY FOR IRISH INDEPENDENCE WON BY PEACEFUL, PARLIAMENTARY MEANS

On 18 September 2014, Scotland went to the polls to decide if it wanted complete independence. They were exercising full, national self-determination. That came about because, for the past number of years, Scotland has had a home rule government and a home rule parliament, and a majority in that parliament was democratically won by a party that wanted complete independence. That could have happened in Ireland too – ninety years ago.

The experience of home rule, of making their own laws in Scotland, of administering their own services and making their own policies, has given the Scots the self-confidence, and the international credibility, to freely consider moving now to full independence. All that has happened in Scotland without the loss of life, without the bitterness of war.

Ireland was given a similar opportunity – to move through home rule, towards ever greater independence, gradually and peacefully – when home rule for Ireland became law on 18 September 1914.

We won that opportunity by parliamentary means and without the loss of a life.

We chose, for various reasons which I will explore, not to follow that path. But the fact that we won the opportunity to take it, and won it by parliamentary methods, should be celebrated by this parliamentary democracy one hundred years later.

Given that this *is* a parliamentary democracy, one of the oldest surviving ones in Europe, and one that did not descend into totalitarianism during the twentieth century, it is important that we should celebrate parliamentary achievements. Remembering democratic, non-violent achievements should be part of the civic education of our nation.

The passage into law of home rule for Ireland was, as I have said, an Irish parliamentary achievement without equal in the preceding two hundred years.

It granted Ireland its own legislature, something denied it since 1800. It was of comparable importance to the land acts, also achieved by diligent parliamentary work, and peaceful agitation – and achieved by the same people.

Given that the Home Rule Act of 1914 provided Ireland with a right – one that had been denied for the previous 114 years – to an Irish legislature meeting in Ireland, the centenary of its passage into law should be specially marked in our legislature, in the Dáil and Seanad Éireann.

The 1916 rebellion, the warfare of the 1919 to 1923 period that it engendered, and indeed of the Great War as well, are all to be commemorated. That is good.

But if these commemorations of violent events are not seen to be accompanied by a balancing and equally high-profile commemoration of peaceful parliamentary achievements like home rule, that would glorify military activity at the expense of less glamorous, but contemporarily more relevant, peaceful parliamentary struggle. Such a choice would be saying that killing and dying is something that will be remembered by future generations, but patient peaceful achievements will be quietly forgotten.

As it is today, Ireland in 1914 was a divided society; an emotionally divided island with a majority (mainly of one religious tradition) favouring a large measure of independence, and a strong minority (mainly of another religious tradition) opposing this and favouring integration in the United Kingdom.

In emotionally divided societies it is vital that commemorations be used to learn useful contemporary lessons from history, not merely to celebrate one protagonist or another, or to freshen up old divisions.

Tough but non-violent tactics were needed to win home rule
The enactment of home rule may have been a purely peaceful achievement, but this is not to suggest that those who obtained it, the Irish Parliamentary Party of John Redmond and John Dillon, were mild-mannered and non-confrontational.

Two previous attempts to obtain home rule had failed; one because it was defeated in the House of Commons and the other because it was vetoed in the House of Lords.

To get home rule onto the statute book, the Irish Parliamentary leaders had to get a majority for home rule in the House of Commons, and simultaneously to get British constitutional arrangements changed to remove the House of Lords' power of veto. There was a permanent majority against home rule in the House of Lords, and the veto could only be removed with the consent of the House of Lords itself.

Furthermore, in the House of Commons, the Liberal Party, which had been committed to home rule under Gladstone, had moved away from that policy under his successors, Lord Rosebery, Sir Henry Campbell-Bannerman and Herbert Asquith. In order to secure home rule by peaceful and constitutional methods, the Liberal Party had first to be won back to a firm commitment to pass home rule.

In a masterly exercise of parliamentary leverage and constructive opportunism, Redmond and Dillon achieved both goals in a very short space of time.

They withheld support for the radical 1909 Budget, unless and until there was a commitment to remove the Lords' veto and introduce home rule. They also, in effect, exerted pressure on the King, because the Lords eventually only passed the legislation in response to the threat of the King swamping the House of Lords with a flood of new peers.

All this was achieved from the position of being a minority party in the House, albeit a party whose votes were needed to avoid a general election which the Liberal government feared they would lose. Considerable brinksmanship was needed because if the Irish Parliamentary Party overplayed their hand, the government fell, and Liberals then lost the resultant general election, the cause of home rule would also be lost.

Redmond and Dillon did not have all the trump cards. They just played the cards they had very well indeed.

On the other side of the House, the Irish Parliamentary Party faced a Conservative Party that was so determined to force a general election that they were prepared to incite Ulster Unionists to military insurrection, and to connive with elements in the British military to ensure that the insurrection would not be prevented.

In Britain itself, home rulers had to overcome deep anti-Irish and (as Ronan Fanning has shown in his book *Fatal Path*) anti-Catholic sentiment in some sections – including within the Liberal Party.

Financial gaps also had to be bridged. Unlike Scotland today, Ireland in 1914 had no oil. Between 1896 and 1911, British government expenditure in Ireland (including recently introduced old age pensions) had increased by 91%, whereas revenue raised in Ireland had risen by only 28%. That enduring gap between spending commitments and revenue explains why the Irish Free State had to take a shilling off the old age pension in the 1920s.

In the face of all these difficulties, getting home rule onto the statute book, without the loss of a single life, was a remarkable parliamentary achievement.

If commemorations are about drawing relevant lessons for today's generation from the work of past generations, this remarkable exercise of parliamentary leverage, to achieve radical reform against entrenched resistance, has much greater relevance to today's generation of democrats, than does the blood sacrifice of Pearse and Connolly.

The subsequent turning away from constitutional methods after 1916 has obscured the scale of this parliamentary achievement. There may have been a fear that too much praise of the prior constitutional achievement would delegitimise the subsequent blood sacrifice.

The Woodenbridge speech

The Woodenbridge speech of John Redmond on 20 September 1914, urging Irish men to join the Allied cause in the Great War that had broken out six weeks previously, must be seen in the context that home rule had been placed on the statute book just two days previously.

Home rule was law, but the implementation of it was postponed until the end of what most people expected would be a short war.

Redmond's address to the Volunteers at Woodenbridge was not a mere reciprocation of the passage of home rule. He also wanted to show that the passage of home rule had inaugurated a new and better relationship between Ireland and its neighbouring island.

He wanted to show everybody, including Ulster Unionists, that things had changed. As he was still aiming to persuade Ulster Unionists to come in under home rule, he felt he needed to do this if there was to be any chance at all that they would voluntarily do so. He wanted to show the Ulster Unionists that, in some matters, Unionists and Nationalists were now 'on the same side'.

Let us not forget that Irish men had fought in the British Army during the Boer War, notwithstanding Redmond and the Irish Parliamentary Party's opposition to that war, so many of those who volunteered to fight in what turned out to be the Great War would have done so anyway, whether Redmond asked them to do so or not.

What would have happened if Redmond had given a different speech at Woodenbridge, vocally opposing recruitment?

He would have handed a powerful argument to those who had opposed home rule all along, namely the argument that a Dublin home rule government could not be trusted not to undermine Britain's international position at a time of great danger.

Carson and Craig, and their allies in the British Conservative Party, would then have felt themselves entirely vindicated in their opposition to home rule.

The Woodenbridge speech also stood on its own merits. The unprovoked invasion by Germany of a small neutral country, Belgium, in order better to be able to attack France, was something that many people at the time, and since, regarded as profoundly wrong and deserving to be opposed.

That said, the Great War was an avoidable tragedy and a failure of statesmanship. But it was not a failure for which Redmond or the Irish Parliamentary Party were responsible. They had to deal with the situation as they found it.

It is right to commemorate the Irish dead of the Great War, but home rule's passage into law is a separate matter. It should be commemorated on its own merits, and separately. It is not a mere addendum to the remembrance of the Great War, but a unique parliamentary achievement.

Parnell did not get home rule onto the statute book. Redmond and Dillon did.

O'Connell did not succeed in re-establishing by law an Irish legislature, Redmond and Dillon did.

Were the powers granted by home rule too little?
Some have criticised the limitations of the Home Rule Act of 1914. These limitations can be explained by the fact that, although the possibility of the temporary exclusion of some Ulster counties had been conceded by the time home rule finally came to be enacted, the Act had been framed from the outset in terms that could apply to all thirty-two counties of Ireland, where there was a Catholic majority, so safeguards and understandable limitations had to be inserted to protect and reassure the Protestant minority in Ulster and elsewhere in Ireland.

For example, a provision was inserted whereby the home rule government 'could not endow any religion'. This safeguard was actually a worry to the Catholic hierarchy, who feared it might affect existing state funding for Catholic teacher training colleges.

For a similar reason, marriage law was to be kept at Westminster, because the Vatican's *Ne Temere* decree of 1907 on mixed marriages had caused alarm among Protestants.

Likewise, limitations on the imposition of tariffs and duties were needed to reassure the large industrial sector in Ulster that their interests would not be sacrificed to the needs of the predominantly agricultural interests that dominated the rest of the country.

As it transpired, these safeguards were not enough. Ulster Unionists continued to insist on exclusion from the whole system, and backed their demand with the threat of force. They were encouraged in this by the Conservative opposition in Westminster.

If John Redmond had wanted to maximise the powers of the home rule government in Dublin, he could, early on, have accepted the exclusion from home rule of the Ulster counties where there was a Unionist majority. This is what the Irish state subsequently did. Even the Conservatives would have given Redmond such a deal. Under such a deal, the exclusion might have been limited to four Ulster counties – instead of six, as in 1921.

But Redmond was unwilling to accept any open-ended exclusion from home rule of any part of Ireland. In that sense, John Redmond was more idealistic than the republicans who came after him.

In January 1914, at the height of the Ulster resistance to home rule, John Redmond was speaking at a meeting in his constituency in Waterford about the difficulty of winning over Ulster Unionists, when a heckler shouted up at him, 'We are as well off without them.' Redmond replied indignantly, 'No, we are not. That is an absolute fallacy.'

The American historian, Joseph P. Finnan, in his book *John Redmond and Irish Unity, 1912–1918*, said that Redmond prized Irish unity more than he prized Irish sovereignty.

He added, 'Although he [Redmond] acceded to demands for temporary exclusion of northern counties, he never gave them up for lost. The Irish revolutionaries who negotiated the Anglo–Irish Treaty of 1921 did just that. Even the anti-treaty forces led by de Valera based their objections on the loss of the republican ideal, not the loss of the northern nationalist population.'

The Cork-based supporter of the Irish Parliamentary Party, J.J. Horgan, said much the same thing in his 1949 memoir, *Parnell to Pearse*. His book concludes with these words: 'We constitutionalists had been wisely prepared to make large concessions in order to avoid the division of our country which we believed to be the final and intolerable wrong. The price of our successors' triumph was Partition … They sacrificed Irish unity for Irish sovereignty.'

A sovereign thirty-two county state was not achieved in 1921, but the 'freedom to achieve freedom' for twenty-six counties – no more than was available to Redmond in 1914.

Those who came after Redmond, using the gun, did not bring unity any closer than he did.

Perhaps the two communities on this island are too different, in their sense of deepest identity, for that.

The 1916 Rising and its impact on possible unity
Charles Townsend, in his book *Easter 1916*, stated, 'The Rebellion played a part in cementing partition.'

Indeed, the words of the Proclamation were literally 'oblivious' to the problem of resistance, in parts of Ulster, to any form of rule by Dublin, notwithstanding Pearse's professed admiration for the UVF arming itself to resist even a modest measure of home rule.

The 1916 Proclamation said it was 'oblivious of the differences carefully fostered by an alien government, who have divided a minority from a majority in the past'.

In effect, they did not think the Ulster Unionists had minds of their own, but were simply tools of the British. Apart from rhetoric, no attempt was made to persuade them of the merits of an Irish Republic, nor thought given to how such persuasion might be done.

Whereas Redmond had tried to talk to Carson and Craig, the 1916 leaders were, preoccupied with the gaining of a republic, at the cost of excluding Ulster.

The irreversibility of home rule
When the decision to use physical force was made by the leaders of the IRB and the Irish Citizen Army in April 1916, home rule was already law. Its implementation was postponed for the duration of the war, but there was little doubt that it would come into effect once the war was over, either for the whole of Ireland, or, more likely, for twenty-six or twenty-eight counties.

The irreversibility of home rule is well illustrated by a comment that had been made by one of its staunchest opponents, the Conservative leader Andrew Bonar Law. He had admitted, 'If Ulster, or rather any county, had the right to remain outside the Irish Parliament, for my part my objection would be met.'

This comment shows that home rule could easily have led to an even larger measure of independence for the rest of Ireland, so long as some Ulster counties were allowed to opt out of it.

As to the irreversibility of home rule, Lloyd George's coalition government's re-election manifesto in the December 1918 election stated bluntly, 'Home rule is upon the statute book.' There was thus no going back on home rule as far as the Conservative and Liberal politicians who wrote that manifesto were concerned.

I believe that, at that time, instead of launching a policy of abstention from Parliament and a guerrilla war, Sinn Féin and the IRA should have used the Home Rule Act as a peaceful stepping stone to dominion status and full independence, in the same way that the treaty of 1921 was so used. They might not have secured more than twenty-eight counties, but there would have been no more bloodshed.

Was 1916 a 'just war'?
Many of the 1916 leaders were familiar with Catholic teaching on what constitutes a 'just war'. One of the criteria is that war should be a last resort. Another is that it should have a reasonable chance of success.

The fact that home rule was passed, would have come into effect at the end of the Great War, and would have been a platform for further moves towards greater independence, shows that the use of violence in 1916 was not a genuine last resort, and thus did not meet that criterion for a just war.

Moreover, the 1916 leaders accepted they had no chance of military success when they marched out on Easter Monday, 1916.

Was alliance with Germany wise?
Another important context in which the 1916 decision must be judged is that of the Great War, in which thousands of Irish soldiers were fighting on the Allied side when the GPO was occupied by force.

The 1916 leaders explicitly took the opposite side in this war to their fellow Irishmen in the trenches.

In proclaiming the Republic, the 1916 leaders spoke of their 'gallant allies in Europe'. These allies were the German Empire, the Ottoman Empire and the Austro–Hungarian Empire. Although their immediate target was Britain, those the Irish Republicans went to war with also included Belgium and the French Republic, whose territory had been pre-emptively invaded and occupied by force, by Germany.

The 1916 leaders were not neutral. They took the side of Germany, Turkey and Austria-Hungary, and said so in their own Proclamation.

This stance greatly weakened the position of Irish negotiators, including Sean T. O'Kelly, who sought to get a hearing at the 1919 Paris Peace Conference for the case for Irish independence. The 1916 leaders' decision had put them on the wrong side, and had made them 'allies', in the words of the Proclamation, of the losers in the Great War.

This was complicated by the fact that the Irish Republic had already been declared anyway, regardless of the Peace Conference. The Irish delegation was not making a claim; it was looking for a retrospective vindication of its pre-existing declaration of a Republic.

As Charles Townshend put it in his book, *The Republic: The Fight for Irish Independence*: 'The Peace Conference would now be asked not to investigate and adjudicate on a national claim, but to recognise an already existing Republic, approving an act hostile to a great power [Britain].'

The fact that a Republic had been declared anyway in 1916, and again in 1919, made winning support for any subsequent compromise – short of the ideal Republic of thirty-two counties – much more difficult, as the treaty negotiators were to find. This absolutism ruled out compromise.

It would have been wiser to have had patience, avoided violence, and adhered to the home rule policy and constitutional methods.

Home rule – a better deal for Northern Nationalists
I concede that the home rule policy would likely not have led to a united thirty-two-county Ireland in the medium or perhaps even the long term – although John Redmond and his colleagues would probably not have accepted that at the time.

The opposition to being under a Dublin home rule parliament was so strong among Unionists in Ulster that, no matter how hard the home rulers might have tried to persuade them, at least four Ulster counties would have stayed out of the Dublin parliament.

The leader of the Irish Party, John Redmond himself, told the House of Commons that 'no coercion shall be applied to any single county in Ireland to force them against their will to come into the Irish government'.

John Redmond's policy was one of attempting to persuade Unionists to accept a united Ireland, and his support for recruitment to the British Army in 1914 was part of that.

This was a sensible policy.

Irish attempts to coerce Northern Ireland into a united Ireland, whether by the attempted incursions across the border in 1922, by the propaganda campaign in the late 1940s, or by IRA killing campaigns in the 1950s and from 1969 to 1998, have all failed miserably, because they were based on a faulty analysis of reality. Likewise attempts to persuade the British to do the job for us, and to use their military and economic force to coerce Unionists into a United Ireland, were also failures. Only when all forms of coercion towards a united Ireland were abandoned did progress eventually become possible, in the 1990s.

Under the home rule arrangement, if Ulster counties opted out of home rule, they would have continued under direct rule from Westminster. There would have been no Stormont parliament, no 'Protestant parliament for a Protestant people', no B Specials, no gerrymandering of local government.

Stormont was not part of the home rule arrangement, and it came about largely because the abstention of Sinn Féin from the Irish Convention and from Parliament after the 1918 election created an opening for it. There was then no Irish nationalist voice to object to it in Westminster.

Under home rule, there would instead have been continued, but reduced, Irish representation at Westminster, so any attempts to discriminate against the nationalist minority in the excluded area of Ulster would have been preventable in a way that was not possible under the eventual settlement. Stormont was left to its own devices after 1921.

The constitutional home rule policy would thus have been much better for Northern Nationalists than the policy of violent separatism was to prove to be.

Northern Nationalists probably sensed this. While the rest of Ireland was plumping for Sinn Féin in the election of December

1918, the electors of West Belfast chose to elect Joe Devlin of the Irish Parliamentary Party to represent them in preference to Éamon de Valera of Sinn Féin.

Sticking with the home rule policy would have saved thousands of lives
The home rule path would also have been better because it would have saved many lives throughout Ireland. People who died between 1916 and 1923 would have survived and would instead have contributed to Irish life, rather than to Irish martyrology.

All things being equal, in my opinion, living for Ireland is better than dying (or killing) for Ireland.

I would emphasise that the waste of these lost lives needs to be weighed, and weighed heavily, in the balance against any supposed advantages secured by the use of force.

There is a moral issue here. Irish people today take the ending of life seriously. 1916, and the subsequent campaigns of violence it inspired, involved ending thousands of lives. Any commemorations should take those valuable lost lives, all of them, into account.

Remember all who died, on both sides, and no side
262 Irish civilians died during the 1916 rebellion, some at the hands of the rebels and many as a result of British artillery designed to expel the rebels from the positions they had occupied.

These civilians did not have any say in the IRB/Citizen Army action, and would all have lived if the Rising had not taken place. They did not volunteer for the sacrifice they made.

We know of the rebels who died, and their deaths have been commemorated by the Irish state. Each year the Irish Army has a Mass to pray for the souls of those who 'died for Ireland' in 1916. It is unclear to me whether this formula includes the civilians who did not decide to put their lives at risk 'for Ireland', but who were killed anyway because they were in the wrong place at the wrong time.

153 soldiers in British Army uniforms were killed in the fighting in Dublin in 1916. Of these, 52 of the dead were Irish, including:

Gerald Neilan from Roscommon; Francis Brennan from Ushers Island in Dublin; Abraham Watchorn from Rathvilly, Co. Carlow; John Brennan from Gowran, Co. Kilkenny; and John Flynn from Carrick-on-Suir. I hope the 100th anniversary of their deaths will not be forgotten the year after next.

Three members of the unarmed Dublin Metropolitan Police were killed, as were fourteen members of the RIC, including Patrick Leen from Abbeyfeale, Co. Limerick and Patrick Brosnan from Dunmanway, Co. Cork.

These Irish men were acting on the orders of a duly constituted government, elected by a parliament that had already granted home rule to Ireland, and to which Ireland had democratically elected its own MPs.

Did these men not 'die for Ireland' too? How should they, and their sacrifice, be remembered? These are questions which need to be answered between now and 2016.

Consider also the dead of the War of Independence from 1919 to 1921 and the dead of the Civil War of 1922 to 1923, for these deaths flowed, in some measure, from the initial decision to use force in 1916.

1,200 were killed in the war of 1919 to 1921. Many of these were civilians who had not chosen the path of war. Others were policemen, who had chosen that vocation as a service to their people, not to become participants in a war. Some casualties were supposed or actual informers on behalf of either side.

Had there been no 'blood sacrifice' in 1916, had there been no executions, had the British government not mishandled conscription in 1918, and had the Home Rule Party (Irish Parliamentary Party) not been rejected by the electorate in the general election of December 1918 in favour of a policy of abstention and separatism, home rule would have come into effect and all those people would have lived.

Many families of minority religions were made to feel unwelcome in Ireland as a result of the violence, and some of these families left. Southern Ireland became a less diverse society as a result of the policy of violence initiated by IRB and the Citizen Army at Easter of 1916.

And of course, around 4,000 Irish people were killed in the Civil War. Like those who were killed in the 1916 to 1921 period, many of these were amongst the brightest talents of their generation.

The sacrifice of the dead made compromise harder
Violence breeds violence. Sacrifice breeds intransigence. The dead exert an unhealthy power over the living, persuading the living to hold out for the impossible, lest the sacrifice of the dead be perceived to have been in vain.

In that sense, the policy of violence initiated in April 1916 contributed to the Civil War of 1922–3. The earlier deaths of those who occupied the General Post Office in 1916, in defence of a thirty-two-county Republic proclaimed a few days before, made it so much harder for those on the anti-treaty side, who occupied the Four Courts in 1922, to accept anything less than a thirty-two-county Republic. They did not want to appear to 'betray' the dead by accepting any compromise. This was unfortunate and mistaken, but understandable.

Betrayal of the sacrifices of the dead is one of the most emotionally powerful, and destructive, accusations within the canon of romantic nationalism. It exercised its baleful influence again in recent times in delaying the abandonment by the IRA of its failed and futile campaign to coerce and bomb Unionists into a United Ireland.

Home rule would have led to dominion status, and to the sort of independence now enjoyed by Canada, Australia and New Zealand
I believe Ireland would have reached the position it is in today, an independent nation of twenty-six counties, if it had stuck with the home rule policy and if the 1916 rebellion had not taken place. Indeed, we might have been a state of twenty-eight counties. All that was needed was a deal on Ulster.

Like all counter factual historical arguments, this proposition is impossible to prove. But once the Ulster question had been resolved by some form of exclusion of areas with a Unionist majority, the path towards greater independence was wide open.

The stance of the Irish Parliamentary Party in the 1918 election was that of attaining dominion status, and I believe they would have achieved it. Perhaps they would not have achieved it by 1921, as it was achieved in the Anglo–Irish Treaty of that year, but it would probably have been achieved by the end of the 1920s – most likely from a Labour government whose policy already envisaged dominion status for Ireland.

Certainly many of the parties in the home rule parliament would have been demanding greater independence. It is important to remember that the electorate of the Home Rule government, that would have come into being in 1919 for twenty-six or twenty-eight counties if the rebellion had not taken place, would have been much bigger than the one that had voted in previous general elections.

All men, and all woman over thirty, would have had the vote for the new home rule parliament, as they had in the 1918 UK general election. This bigger electorate would have greatly enhanced the electoral prospects of parties, like Labour and Sinn Féin, who would undoubtedly have been demanding progressive increases in the power of the home rule parliament vis-à-vis Westminster. This would have happened ... but without the loss of life.

Irish politics would not have stood still after home rule, as some historians seem to assume. Redmond's party might have won a majority in the first home rule parliament, just as Scottish Labour got the majority in Scotland's first home rule parliament. But subsequent elections might have seen more independence-minded parties win majorities in Dublin in the 1920s or 1930s, just as happened in Scotland under home rule eighty years later.

Once Ireland had its own legislature in Dublin, it would have been able to avail of the progressive loosening of ties within the Empire, in the same way as the Irish Free State was able to do, for example through the Statute of Westminster of 1931. Ireland could have followed Canada, South Africa and Australia's path.

Some might argue that security and defence considerations would have made this unlikely. I doubt that.

If a Conservative-dominated government was willing, in 1938, to hand over the treaty ports to Éamon de Valera, who, twenty-two years previously, had been a declared ally of Germany, it would surely have been willing to place as much trust in a home rule government in Dublin, whose political antecedents had stood with Britain in its moment of greatest threat in 1914.

Conclusion

To say that the 1916 Rising was a mistake is not to deny the heroism or sincerity of those who made the mistake, or the heroism of those who followed them. Hindsight enables us to gain a perspective that may not have been obvious at the time.

But the reality is that in 1916 home rule was on the statute book and was not about to be reversed. If the 1916 leaders had shown more patience, a lot of destruction could have been avoided, and I believe we would still have achieved the independence we enjoy today.

Based on an address given on 18 September 2014 at a seminar organised by the Reform Group, in the Royal Irish Academy, Dame Street, Dublin, marking the exact centenary of the passage into law, for the first time ever, of an Irish Home Rule Act (18 September 1914).

A VISIT TO THE BATTLEFIELDS OF THE SOMME

In August 2013, I visited the battlefields of the Somme in northern France.

During the First World War a number of battles were fought in this area, but the most important of these commenced on 1 July 1916 with a joint Franco–British offensive, and lasted until November 1916.

50,000 French soldiers, 95,000 British and Commonwealth soldiers, and 164,000 German soldiers were killed.

Despite their heavy casualties, the Allies gained only a dozen square miles of territory.

Although launched to make a big breakthrough, the Allied offensive became a battle of attrition, wearing out German resources of men and material, and in that it was partially successful. The offensive on the Somme tied up German troops, relieving pressure elsewhere, notably on the French at Verdun, and on Russia in the east.

Artillery fire was more devastating than face-to-face combat. Artillery accounted for 58% of all casualties, rifle and machine-gun fire for 39%, and bayonets for just 0.3%.

A large number of the 49,000 Irish who died in the Great War did so at the Somme.

One of those who died there, in September 1916, was Tom Kettle, an officer in the Royal Dublin Fusiliers. He was Professor of Economics in UCD, and had served as an Irish Parliamentary Party MP for East Tyrone. Shortly before his death, he had written, 'I am calm and happy, but desperately anxious to live. If I live I mean to spend the rest of my life working for perpetual peace. I have seen war, and faced modern artillery, and I know what an outrage it is against simple men.'

A colleague wrote of him to his wife after his death, 'He died for Ireland and for Europe.'

The battlefields today are sparsely populated, open, rolling countryside. Apart from the memorials and the rows of white and grey crosses, it is hard to believe that the area could ever have been a place of industrial-scale slaughter.

I visited the modest memorial in Guillemont to the 16th Irish Division, in which Tom Kettle served. Although almost all those who served in that division were from what is now the Republic of Ireland, all the poppy wreaths I saw there had been laid by groups from Northern Ireland.

I also saw the much larger Ulster Tower, which commemorates the 36th Ulster Division, many of whose members had been drawn from the Unionist Ulster Volunteers. Finally, I visited the Newfoundland trenches, from which the Newfoundland Regiment launched an attack on the first day of the battle, in which almost every soldier died.

If anyone still needs convincing that we need institutions in place to maintain unity and peace in Europe, he or she should visit the Somme.

IRELAND AND EUROPE – 1814, 1914 AND 2014:
HISTORY AS SEEN THROUGH THE LIFE OF
CLONGOWES WOOD COLLEGE

∽

A commemoration can enable a society, a country, or a school to reaffirm its separate identity. That can be good, but it can also be bad, if it makes others feel excluded or undervalued.

The best commemorations are the ones which help us to learn what the past was really like, not just for our own ancestors, but for others, who may have had a different life experience from our ancestors, or may even have been their enemies or opponents.

Learning about others, and their life experiences, over the distance of time and geography, is a fundamental part of commemoration, and of education.

All commemoration, like all historical study, should be revisionist – even revising the revisionists themselves!

2014 was a particularly important year for commemorations – 1914 saw the start of the Great War at the beginning of August, and the passage into law, a month later, of an Irish Home Rule Bill.

1814 was also a notable year. France was defeated by the Allies, and Napoleon had to abdicate. The Apprentice Boys were founded in Derry, the Royal Dublin Society bought Leinster House, there was a major fraud in the London Stock Exchange, and the Great Beer Flood took place in London, when hundreds of thousands of gallons of beer escaped from a vat and drowned two people. And Clongowes Wood College was founded.

In some respects, 1814 and 1914 each initiated a new European order. The Allied victory in 1814, confirmed a year later at Waterloo, brought into being, at the Congress of Vienna, a conservative inter-state system based on consultations and maintenance of a balance of power. The revolutionary era, in which France sought to remake Europe by force, was thus ended. Europe settled into a period of relative peace, and of small, fairly contained, wars; an era that lasted exactly one hundred years, until 1914.

The new European order initiated in July/August 1914 was very different. A complex set of two rival alliances, designed in the early twentieth century to give participant nations security, became instead a source of massive insecurity. The rival alliance systems of the summer of 1914 eventually drew all the major nations of Europe (except Spain) into war against one another, all over a quarrel between Austria-Hungary and Serbia, in which the rest of Europe had virtually no interest.

It was a bit like the financial crash of 2008, when complex financial instruments, designed to increase security by spreading risk, actually dragged everybody down. The risk was spread too widely, as were the alliances, and the fragility of the whole interdependent system was exposed.

The 1914 era lasted seventy-six years. The Great War was the source of two other wars, the Second World War and the Cold War, the latter of which only unwound in 1990.

1814 in Ireland was the last year of a long war, dating from 1790, in which this country had been intimately involved. A rebellion in 1798, the Act of Union, and the undelivered promise of Catholic Emancipation were all outgrowths of that conflict, as was the participation of Irish soldiers in Wellington's victory at Waterloo the following year. 40% of his 'British' Army were Irish.

Ireland's economy had boomed during the war, as it did during the First World War.

But once the war ended, the demand for Irish exports of woollen and cotton goods fell, as new competitors were able to enter its markets. Bank failures were endemic in those years. Agricultural prices collapsed, and evictions were made easier by a law passed in 1816. The average rent was £4 per acre, so the annual rent of 15 acres of land would cover the 50 guinea fee to send a boy to Clongowes for a year. Tithes to the established church, and other property taxes on tenant farmers, were a heavy burden.

Two years after the first boy entered Clongowes, in 1816–17, there was famine across Europe – a year without a summer – the result of a major volcanic eruption in Indonesia, which caused an ash cloud across the northern hemisphere.

Clongowes students entering the school in 1814 would have aspired to careers in the professions – especially law, which was open to Catholics. At this time, however, all the senior judicial posts and senior posts in the public service were filled on the basis of preferment. A Catholic could not become a Senior Counsel or an MP until 1829.

To found the school, the Jesuits were supposed to get a licence from the Protestant bishop. They did not apply, but went ahead anyway – natural risk-takers then as now.

Illiteracy was still very high in Ireland then, though many poor people paid small sums for their children to learn to read and write in 'pay' schools – otherwise known as 'hedge' schools.

Education was a denominational battlefield, with bible societies opening free schools for the poor in the hope of conversions; the Kildare Place Society was committed, at least in principle, to non-denominational schooling, but this was breaking down, and Daniel O'Connell resigned from their boards some years later.

So education, at the time of the founding of Clongowes, would have been a priority for the Catholic Church – and especially the creation of an educational infrastructure for those Catholics who might previously have attended Irish colleges on the Continent, as Daniel O'Connell himself did. O'Connell was able to send his five sons to Clongowes, despite his enormous and chronic debts!

Religious observance was high in Dublin and Leinster, with high mass attendance and a reasonable infrastructure of churches and clergy, although the churches were probably too small to accommodate everybody on Sunday.

In contrast, in the west of Ireland, where the population density was higher, the people were poorer, and church infrastructure and educational provision was much less. Illiteracy was still over 80% in Mayo in 1841, whereas it was under 40% in Kildare, which was better than the European average. Poor people could not afford even a hedge school education.

But it is important to stress that the motive of the Jesuit Fathers coming here two hundred years ago was not primarily educational, political or economic.

Educational, political and economic uplift for Catholics in Ireland may have been secondary goals, goals to which this school contributed enormously, but the primary goal was religious – 'eternal not temporal' *Aeterna non caduca* – to bring the faith to a young generation of people who, through their example, would bring it to others.

The goals of Jesuit education were clear then, as they are now: to assure each person that he or she is known and loved by God, and ought to respond to that, to come to know and understand him or herself, and to make life's decisions from the perspective of others, particularly of the poor.

Jesuit education was, and is, about passing on a faith that does justice in the concrete circumstances of each generation, a faith that helps young people become men and women for others.

That was true in 1814, was true in 1914, and is true, and even more relevant, today.

The Jesuits who came here had been educated in Sicily and other European countries, and brought a continental, even a global, perspective to the education of Irish Catholics. That was true of schools founded later by other orders, like Castleknock and Blackrock.

The wider global perspective of Jesuit education remains true today, and explains why so many Irish graduates of Clongowes, and other Jesuit schools, have contributed so much to global affairs. Freddie Boland, Paddy McGilligan, Garret FitzGerald and Peter Sutherland spring to mind.

Of course, it was not all plain sailing for Clongowes.

When the Intermediate Certificate was introduced in 1878, it was to be the basis for state payments to schools on the strength of results in the exam. When the first results were published in 1879, the upstart Blackrock College got the best results in the country, followed by Tullabeg (subsequently amalgamated with Clongowes), Castleknock, the Royal College in Belfast, and Foyle College in Derry. Clongowes performance was down the line. Clongowes got an unwelcome wake-up call.

Moving forward from 1814 to 1914, we find a very different Ireland, in a very different world. Europe in 1914 was a vastly richer place. In the previous forty years, thanks to dramatic improvements in transport and communications, globalisation, as we would now describe it, had taken place.

People's fate in 1914 was dependent on the decisions of people thousands of miles away, in ways that could not even have been imagined one hundred years previously.

Ireland was the venue of two armed camps: the Irish Volunteers, determined to achieve home rule, and the Ulster Volunteers, determined to prevent it (at least as far as the six north-eastern counties were concerned).

John Redmond, who spoke at Clongowes so eloquently on Union Day on the first of June 1914, was then engaged in tense and very difficult negotiations to bring the Irish Volunteers under the democratic control of the elected representatives of the Irish people, and to avoid an accidental sectarian civil war. He proposed to do so by nominating William Redmond MP (OC 1873–6), Joe Devlin MP, and Dr Michael Davitt to a new governing board of the Irish Volunteers. He succeeded in this goal two weeks later.

He was simultaneously negotiating on how home rule might be modified to accommodate northern Unionists.

He succeeded, three and a half months after he spoke at Clongowes, in having home rule passed into law – the only Irish leader to achieve that, and without a shot having been fired.

He did not achieve a united Ireland, and he was unwilling to use coercion to that end, but those who came after him – using more destructive and coercive methods – have not achieved that goal either. But that is an argument for another time and place.

The international perspective his education at Clongowes had given him may explain how Redmond saw the issues that were at stake in the First World War. He rejected the notion that the Irish people remain neutral, or try to exploit the position in which the war placed Britain and its Allies, France and Belgium, which had been invaded. The invasion was accompanied by well-documented atrocities. Redmond's call for Irish people to volunteer on the Allied side was answered by 604 men who had attended this school, ninety-four of whom were killed.

Today we face a world very different to that of 1914.

This part of Ireland is an independent, sovereign nation, with a historically high standard of living. I was surprised to read recently that, despite austerity and high personal and government debt, and despite the fact that we may not feel better off, consumer spending per head in this state was 40% higher last year than it was in 1997.

But we face a troubled world. A former Czech Foreign Minister recently said that, following the forceful annexation of Crimea by Russia, Europe's long era of peace was over. A European order based on the rule of international law was, he felt, in the process of being replaced by one dominated by spheres of influence by stronger over weaker states, not unlike the world before 1914. But, if that is the way things do go, we will all learn that power politics will be a wasteful, unreliable and dangerous way to organise a world that is now far more interdependent than it was in any other historic era.

It was a pure accident, a volcano on the other side of the globe, that created the climatic conditions that caused the famine in Europe two years after Clongowes was founded, in 1816/17. There was no warning, and no human action could have prevented it.

But if carbon emissions lead to a dramatic rise in sea levels, and in global temperatures, there will have been a warning, and it would have been an avoidable accident.

And those who will suffer most will not be those who caused the problem, but the poorest people in the world, scraping out a living in the drought-prone areas of the world. That is an issue of global justice.

A distorted version of religion, a lack of a better goal in life, and a sense that religious expression is disrespected in some western countries is leading some young European Muslims to involve themselves in sectarian civil wars in the Middle East. That also presents a different, but real, threat to the trusting constitutional order we have become used to in most western countries. And the response to the threat could be as dangerous as the threat itself.

So, rather than simply retreating into a private world of spending and gaining, I hope that it is to issues like these that today's and tomorrow's privileged beneficiaries of a Jesuit-inspired education will turn their minds:

- Constructing and defending a structure of peace in Europe,
- Passing on an undamaged physical environment to the next generation,
- Reconciling faith and reason, and
- Reconciling a good preparation for the next life, with tolerance compassion and justice for others in this one.

These are the challenges I see for the generation of 2014.

They are challenges that are every bit as difficult as those that faced the boys that came here in 1814, and in all the subsequent two hundred years of the school.

Will Clongowes, as a Jesuit-inspired Catholic school, be here in 2114?

The buildings will be here for sure, at least some of them, but what else will still be here of the things we value and celebrate today?

Of course that depends on economic conditions, government rules and so on. Parents will always be willing to pay for the best education they can afford for their children. That's human nature.

The existence of this school, as a Catholic school inspired by Jesuit values, will depend very much on two things:

1. On vocations to the Jesuit order, and/or on the willing commitment of lay people to the values and beliefs that inspire the Order and,
2. On whether the school can visibly and effectively contribute to creating and maintaining an atmosphere that reconciles faith and reason, that does not assume them to be antipathetic to one another, and an atmosphere that reconciles preparation for the next life, with tolerance, generosity towards, and respect for others in this life.

I attended Clongowes Wood College as a student from 1959 to 1965. In the year 2014/2015, the school celebrated the bicentenary of its foundation and I was honoured to be asked to be president of the school's past pupils' union for that year. In that role I gave an address in June 2014 at the school, at one of a series of events marking its bicentenary year. The above article is based on that speech.

I would like to acknowledge the value to me, in preparing the speech, of discussions I had with Professor Mary Daly of UCD, Professor Terry Dooley of NUI Maynooth, and Dr Ciaran O'Neill of Trinity College, whose excellent book Catholics of Consequence *was published by Oxford University Press in 2014.*

I would also like to acknowledge the person who inspired my interest in history – the late Fr Woods SJ. Finally, I wish to remember my Third Line Prefect, Fr Joe Dargan SJ, who sadly died in 2014.

WOODENBRIDGE COMMEMORATION

When John Redmond made his speech calling on Irishmen to join in the effort to repel the German invasion of Belgium and France he was speaking to his friends and neighbours, the men of the East Wicklow Volunteers. He probably would have been personally acquainted with the majority of the men in the parade, and their families.

And on that fateful day, he had been on his way to his home in Aughavanagh.

He had left London a day before, having succeeded in the great task of his life – seeing the Home Rule Bill passed into law, after over thirty years of patient parliamentary work and public peaceful agitation.

He had taken the boat from Holyhead, and was passing Woodenbridge by car and saw the parade taking place under the captaincy of the local schoolmaster and friend of his, a Captain McSweeney, who, in addition to his work as a local teacher and captain in the Volunteers, was a keen activist in the Irish language revival movement.

Having told the men on parade that he knew they would make efficient soldiers, referring to the German invasion of Belgium, John Redmond urged his friends to support the Allied cause as follows: 'Go on drilling and make yourselves efficient for the work, and then account for yourselves as men, not only in Ireland itself, but wherever the fighting line extends in defence of right and freedom and religion in this war.'

Under the Home Rule Bill that had passed into law two days before John Redmond spoke here, an Ireland of thirty-two counties would have had a devolution of the powers of legislation and domestic administration, but without control over foreign and military affairs and without control of customs duties. Any exclusion of Ulster counties was to be purely temporary.

Some have minimised Redmond's achievement in getting home rule passed, criticising his speech two days later in Woodenbridge, and blaming him for Irish casualties in the Great War.

I believe such critics are mistaken.

What John Redmond achieved

John Redmond's achievement was enormous. Relying on wholly constitutional and parliamentary methods, he had succeeded where O'Connell, Butt and Parnell had all failed. He actually got home rule onto the statute book.

After an intense political struggle, in the face of vetoes by the House of Lords, threats of mutiny within the military, and threats of physical violence by the Ulster Volunteers, the Home Rule Bill was finally passed into law on 18 September 1914.

This was a month after the war had broken out with Imperial Germany. When the war first broke out in August 1914, the Asquith-led Liberal government initially wanted to postpone the final passage of the Home Rule Bill, which was still strongly opposed by the Conservative party, as part of a wartime political truce, which was, in Asquith's words, to be 'without prejudice to the domestic and political positions of any party'.

But John Redmond insisted that home rule be brought into law. He got his way. The law was passed, and assented to by the King. However, its operation was suspended for twelve months, or until the end of the war, whichever was to come later. This postponement was seen as reasonable in the circumstances. It allowed the energies of all concerned to be concentrated on winning what was expected to be a short war.

Redmond was right

I believe John Redmond was right about the issues at stake in that war, and in his support for the Allied cause. The German invasion of neutral Belgium the previous month was entirely unprovoked.

Before invading Belgium, Germany had found itself facing a war with Russia over Germany's support of Austro–Hungarian demands on Serbia. Germany was worried that France might go to war in support of Russia. But France had not yet done that.

Imperial Germany did not wait to find out. It decided to attack France first, hoping it could quickly knock out France like it had done in 1870. And the best route by which to attack France was, of course, through Belgium. Belgian neutrality was irrelevant.

Some believe that, as an Irish leader, John Redmond was wrong to takes sides in such a war to defend the territorial integrity of a neutral state. This is a strange position to take, given that we champion our own neutrality today. Perhaps the view is that only our own neutrality is important, that other countries' neutrality does not matter.

That is hardly a sustainable position in international relations.

Redmond was criticised at the time by a minority in the Volunteers, who later seceded, for not waiting for an Irish government to be formed in Dublin before taking sides. But they did not expressly say that it was, as such, wrong for an Irish leader to take a side.

The same people, as rebels in the 1916 Rising, did not wait for an Irish government to be formed, or for a mandate from the people, before taking a side – the opposite side to the one chosen by John Redmond – when they explicitly stated in the Proclamation that their allegiance lay with their 'gallant allies' in Europe.

These 'gallant allies' were Imperial Germany, the Austro–Hungarian Empire and the Ottoman Empire. The morality of this 'alliance' has never been seriously questioned or debated in Ireland in the past century, and perhaps it is time that it was.

Looking at the facts as they were in September 1914 – the unprovoked invasion of neutral Belgium, the excessive demands made on Serbia, and the atrocities committed in Belgium by the Germans – I believe Redmond's position on the war to be more legitimate than the self-proclaimed alliance of the 1916 men with the German, Austro–Hungarian and Ottoman Empires.

I do not believe that the maxim 'your neighbour's difficulty is your opportunity' is necessarily a good one, or one that trumps other considerations. Irish people had then, and have now, a sense of justice, not only for ourselves but for other countries too.

Unity by consent was his goal
Leaving morality aside, was Redmond tactically foolish to call for Irish men to join the British Army in September 1914?

This question has to be judged by what Redmond was trying to achieve at the time. He was trying to persuade Ulster Unionists to voluntarily come in under a home rule government in Dublin.

All the concessions he made, including accepting home rule as a final settlement and accepting a reduction in Irish representation in the House of Commons, were made to achieve that goal – acceptance of home rule by Unionists, or 'unity by consent'.

Redmond believed it was attainable, but only if he could demonstrate to Ulster Unionists that home rule did not mean abandoning their British loyalty. Redmond believed that one way of making Ulster Unionists see Irish Nationalism in a different light, would be if Irish Nationalists stood shoulder to shoulder with them in a common endeavour to defend Belgian neutrality, and the rights of small nations.

Rather than being opponents, as they had been in the previous four years of bitter domestic political struggle, they would thus be on the same side.

Redmond knew he was taking a risk in his call at Woodenbridge. But it was a calculated risk. He took the risk in an attempt to achieve genuine Irish unity.

The methods of achieving unity used by Redmond's critics failed over and over again
Given that all subsequent attempts – including terror, boycotting Northern goods, and demanding that the British coerce Unionists into a united Ireland – have failed to achieve any kind of unity, one should be slow to criticise Redmond.

Of course, if a united Ireland by consent was never a serious goal, and if maximum separation of just twenty-six or twenty-eight counties from Britain was the real goal, one could take a different view.

But that was not John Redmond's position. He believed he could win over Unionists, but he did not believe that would be possible if he stood aside from a conflict that Unionists regarded as existential.

The war was longer than anyone predicted
One might accuse Redmond of making a miscalculation in his speech ninety-eight years ago, because he did not foresee that the war would go on so long. He did not know that there would be so many casualties, and that it would bring down the Liberal government that had made home rule possible in the first place.

At the time most people, including most military experts, expected that this war, like most of the wars of the nineteenth century, would be over within a year or so. Unfortunately they were wrong. Improved defensive military technology (like the machine gun, which made it harder to advance and easier to defend ground), meant that the war dragged on for four and a quarter awful years.

Irish men would have joined the army anyway
It is wrong to hold Redmond responsible for the terrible price that was paid in the trenches. Large numbers of Irish men would have joined up anyway, especially now that home rule was passed, whatever Redmond said or did not say at Woodenbridge; historical evidence clearly points in this direction.

After all, just fourteen years after the passage of the hated Act of Union, 40% of Wellington's army at Waterloo was Irish.

A large number of Irishmen fought in the Crimean War. In his book on that war, *Crimea*, Orlando Figes states that almost one-third of the male population of the parishes of Whitegate and Aghada in East Cork died fighting for the British Army in Crimea.

So to say that Redmond's stance is responsible for the 'terrible price' that a generation of young Irish men paid in the trenches is unhistorical.

The only way Redmond could have affected the issue would have been if he had campaigned for Irish men *not* to join up. But if he had done that, he would have been saying goodbye to Irish unity, and would have run the risk that the Home Rule Act that he had worked so hard to pass would have been repealed on the ground that home rule, in those circumstances, would have been a threat to British security.

It is right to commemorate the introduction of the Home Rule Bill one hundred years ago, in 1912. But introducing the Bill was one thing; passing it and implementing it on an all-Ireland basis was another.

That was what Redmond achieved in September 1914, something which subsequent generations have yet to achieve – the real potential for a united Ireland.

Based on a speech given at a ceremony in Woodenbridge Golf Club, Co. Wicklow, in April 2012, for the unveiling of a stone commemorating the speech of John Redmond MP, leader of the Irish Parliamentary Party, at Woodenbridge in September 1914.

European Union

BETTER LABOUR PRODUCTIVITY IS THE KEY TO EUROPEAN PROSPERITY

Raising productivity should be Europe's top goal for the next ten years
A recent OECD report highlighted low productivity growth as the key challenge facing the European Union. It pointed out that, since 2000, labour productivity in EU countries had risen by only 0.6% per year, whereas the average productivity growth in OECD countries not in the EU was 1.2% per year. Lagging growth of labour productivity is a bigger problem than the debt overhang from the banking crisis. Economic growth deriving from increases in property prices and associated consumer spending is inherently temporary, whereas growth derived from productivity increases will last.

If EU countries become more productive, they will generate the revenue to reduce their private and public debts to manageable proportions. But if European productivity remains low, the debts of Europeans will accumulate. Since the crisis, EU countries have focused on reducing costs, but have neglected investments that might boost long-term productivity.

Germany, for example, has a low level of public investment, even though it can borrow very cheaply to invest. In Ireland, public investment is still at two-thirds the level it was in 2007.

Of course, there are problems defining what 'public investment' means. Building an unnecessary extension to a school would be deemed an 'investment', while employing someone to provide early childhood education would be deemed to be current spending. Yet the spending on early childhood education would probably give a bigger boost to the ultimate productivity of the economy than the underused extra school building.

Given that most EU countries will need to make big medium-term increases in government spending to pay pensions and provide healthcare to an ageing population, it is necessary for them to curb deficits now.

Even now, the EU has only 7% of the world's population, but 48% of the world's government social spending.

Life expectancy in the EU is expected to increase from seventy-six years in 2010, to eighty-four years by 2060. This means there will be a longer period during which pensions must be paid and healthcare provided for more people, and the funds will have to come from a proportionately smaller workforce.

However, cutting deficits by reducing genuine investments that would eventually generate greater productivity – and thus greater revenue to meet those medium-term expenses – would be unwise. The challenge is to know which investments will have that long-term effect, and which will simply generate current activity with little lasting effect on future revenue.

One concrete step that could be taken to prioritise genuine investment over current spending would be to amend the EU Stability and Growth Pact, and exempt money used in co-financing investments with the EU from state deficit calculations. The EU has a system which enables it to assess whether investments are genuine ones that will ultimately enhance the revenue of the state.

The number of people of employable age in the EU will peak in 2022 at 217 million. After that, the number will fall. So if tax revenues and services are to be maintained, productivity must be continually improved.

The productivity of an economy is determined by the efficiency of the entire economy, not just of the export sector.

If government services, the professions, the courts, or the transport system use people's time inefficiently, that can do just as much damage as lack of research or unduly high wages in the export sector.

Ireland, in particular, needs to look at the productivity of its health services, its training systems, and its legal system. All of these sectors appear to be performing relatively poorly by international comparison, and are shielded from external competition.

In Germany, the delays in setting up a new business are a big barrier to improved productivity. Germany is 114th in the global rankings on this, behind Tajikistan and Lesotho. Regulation of professional services is stricter in Germany than in all but five other OECD countries. As a result, notwithstanding its export successes, overall productivity in the German economy is growing slower than is the case in Portugal.

Full-scale EU-wide competition in the services sector is key to solving this problem of weak labour productivity. This will enable Europe to maintain living standards, despite the decline in the working population relative to the retired population they will have to support.

THE EUROPEAN UNION MUST DEVELOP A PATRIOTISM OF ITS OWN

The European Union will only survive the dramatic changes the twenty-first century will bring if the citizens of all EU states develop a common sense of European patriotism alongside their national patriotisms.

Appeals to monetary self-interest and rational calculation alone will not be enough to keep the Union together in the face of a new world dominated by Asian economic power.

European patriotism, like national patriotism, is not something that will arise spontaneously. It has to be fostered by the use of symbols and appeals to people's emotions, and by political leaders who make a conscious decision to do so. This is not merely a matter for information campaigns and advertising. It is a matter for political leadership.

The sixtieth anniversary of the Schuman Declaration fell on 9 May 2010. That declaration launched the project that has since become the European Union. It is also the date of an important election in the German state of North Rhine-Westphalia.

How does the European Union stand sixty-five years on,

- After an unprecedented enlargement to twenty-eight members?
- After agreeing on a new constitutional arrangement , democratically approved by all twenty-eight countries?
- After fifteen years of its own currency – the euro?

Are the electors of Europe proud of what they have achieved?

Do they even think about it at all, or do they just take it for granted?

Are they proud of the fact that, despite being told from the very beginning that democratically pooling sovereignty was hopelessly naive, and despite being told that Europe was suffering a problem called 'eurosclerosis', the EU has grown to 350 million people, has signed a new treaty, and the euro is holding its own?

Are they proud that Europe has created the only truly voluntary and democratic union of states in human history?
I am afraid the answer to all those questions is no. No they are not particularly proud of it, because they are rarely told by their timorous political leaders that they should be proud of it.

So we should not be surprised if electorates in important elections, like the one in Westphalia, think only of their own country's interests.

Unless the European Union's citizens come to be proud of their Union, the Union will not survive the twenty-first century.

A Union whose base is solely in its technocratic achievements, and not in the hearts of its citizens, will not be capable of withstanding any existential challenge that the twenty-first century might throw at it.

Indecision on the euro is a symptom of a deeper lack of popular belief
A lack of popular belief is why so many countries that are net contributors to the EU budget focus on ways to get their money back, and why one country even has a special rebate.

That is why we have not had clear and prompt decision making on a loan for the new Greek government to help it clean up the mess it inherited. Instead of seeing this as a European problem, to which a European solution must be found, we have had a series of national political calculations which ignore the mutual interest we all have in overcoming the Greek problem.

An attempt to solve the Greek financial problem has to wait until after an election in North Rhine-Westphalia because an insufficient effort has been made to explain to the intelligent electors of that large German state that sorting out the Greek problem quickly, before the election, is in their interests for three reasons.

First, because the euro has been vitally helpful to Germany in increasing its exports, keeping its exchange rate at a more competitive level than it would have been if Germany was still using the Deutsche Mark.

Second, because it protects German banks who have bought a lot of Greek bonds.

Third, because the euro is at the heart of EU integration, and a failure of the euro would deprive Germany of economic influence over its key markets.

Europe needs a political leadership in every member state that is willing to explain that Europe's mutual interests are superior to the interests of individual states, and that we will all gain, both materially and morally, by staying together and building the 'ever closer union' sought in the Treaty of Rome so long ago.

Based on a speech to the Institute of International and European Affairs (IIEA), delivered in Brussels in April 2010, before the first Greek bailout was agreed. Though these words were written in 2010, they are as valid now as they were then. Public opinion in Germany, and in other EU countries, still looks too often at European problems through a myopically national lens, lacking a true European patriotism.

IS THERE SUCH A THING AS EUROPEAN CIVILISATION?
ARE THERE EUROPEAN VALUES?
WHAT UNITES US AS EU CITIZENS?

If Europeans do not have a well understood consensus about what it means to be European, what unites us, what values define us, we will find it increasingly difficult to build the sort of integrated economic unity that is required by our present economic situation.

This is because values and economics cannot be separated.

A recently published European Values Survey, conducted in all European countries, shows that Europeans have widely divergent views about what constitutes a good life, about mutual obligations, and about individualism and community. When approaching common EU questions, each nation will tend to assume its approach is best, or indeed the only valid one, and may be quite uninformed about what others think and why.

There is no common conversation in Europe about the things that are important. That is not a recipe for harmony and unity.

The concept of EU citizenship goes back to the Maastricht Treaty in 1992 (Article 17 of current EU treaties).

A promise of common citizenship implies a shared set of values that encompasses shared rights, and therefore, as the treaties say, shared obligations and responsibilities.

A right without a corresponding obligation is a logical impossibility. If someone has a right, some other person or group has to be on hand – and willing – to ensure that it is vindicated.

The concept of European civilisation goes back even further than that of a shared citizenship.

Europeans once felt comfortable invading other parts of the

world because they felt they had something special, knowledge or a set of values, that they could bring to those parts of the world. This was the notion of Europe's 'civilising mission'. This notion was used to justify colonialism.

The idea was that Europe could bring some good things to other parts of the world that would not enter there without some form of compulsion, and that the benefits of these good things would exceed the costs.

Of course, there were selfish reasons too, and a great deal of brutality, racism, and exploitation. But some Europeans, at least, were able to live with their consciences because they felt they were, ultimately, doing good in the countries they colonised.

Colonialism is now, thankfully, over. So the question arises – do Europeans still have a shared set of values and norms that can contribute positively to the world?

The construction of the European Union, going right back to the 1950s, proceeds from the assumption that Europeans share a set of values strong enough to allow a pooling of sovereignty.

It also presumes the existence of some form of shared European civilisation that distinguishes Europeans, to some degree at least, from Asians, North Americans, Africans, and South Americans, in the same way that individual nations within Europe have shared values that distinguish them from one another.

Some might sum up these 'European Values' as democracy and the rule of law. But democracy and the rule of law will only suffice as binding agents for Europe if there is a minimal understanding across Europe of what they mean in practice. That is not something that can be delegated to lawyers in the European Court of Human Rights. Lawyers can only do their job well, and without hubris, if there is a minimum consensus on basic questions like these.

- What should the law say?
- How far should majority views, in a democracy, intrude on private lives?
- Should people be treated exclusively as individuals, or do families have rights and obligations?
- When does a life become human, and when should it begin to enjoy human rights?

Democracy cannot easily survive if people's views of what should be done collectively are totally divergent, and if there is no underlying consensus. Democracy was brought down in the 1930s in most of Europe because that necessary consensus had ended. That could happen again.

The rule of law will not survive, and laws will not be enforceable in practice, unless there is some shared sense across Europe of what the law should say, of what is private and what is public, and of how far law should go in regulating the former.

Elites cannot go too far beyond the consensus in society when imposing their views on what the law should say, through the courts in Europe or nationally. This is especially so in a Europe of five hundred million people, where so many different viewpoints exist.

If we are to create a society in the European Union based on shared and mutually enforced values, we need to establish whether or not such shared European values really exist. We need some mechanism for discussing these values with one another, across Europe, in a mutually respectful way.

It cannot be a matter of those countries (or groups) who believe themselves to be more advanced, more enlightened, enforcing their values on those they deem to be lesser.

That will not work, and will eventually provoke a reaction, and almost certainly one that will not be welcome. We have already seen, in Hungary, an EU country which proclaims itself to be an 'illiberal democracy'.

On 19 June 2013, the French newspaper *Le Monde* reported on a recently published European Values Study which showed dramatic differences between Europeans in what they believe should be the role of society, and the role of the individual.

The study chose nineteen indicators to measure how 'individualised' the values of countries were, and thus what they believed the role of the individual ought to be. The study covered Europeans in all forty-seven European countries, not just the European Union. It also covered the area of the Council of Europe, and the European Convention on Human Rights, which the Council generated.

Among the indices of individualisation were the following:

- Adherence to a relativist value system, rather than one based on a set of principles,
- A belief that one expresses and develops oneself primarily through paid work (as distinct from family responsibilities),
- A belief that one should spend one's leisure time according to personal taste,
- A belief that one should choose one's form of family, with each member of a couple having a separate set of friends, choosing whether or not to have children, choosing to marry or not,
- A belief that homosexual couples should adopt children,
- A belief in liberal abortion laws,
- Tolerance of divorce, adultery, euthanasia and suicide.

The survey ranked countries by the proportion of their population that was 'individualised', according to these measures, in 2008.

The most 'individualised' country in Europe is Sweden, where 84% of the population had this (perhaps arbitrarily chosen) set of beliefs that supposedly defined individualism. In contrast with Sweden's 84% preference for individualism, support for that view is only at

- 7% in Cyprus,
- 10% in Malta,
- 19% in Romania,
- 22% in Croatia,
- 24% in Latvia,
- 26% in Greece, and
- 28% in Bulgaria.

Just across the Baltic Sea from Sweden, in Estonia, only 24% had the same opinion as the Swedes. Even closer to Sweden, only 20% were of that opinion in Poland, which means that 80% of Poles did *not* agree with the Swedish view.

After Sweden, the next most 'individualised' country was Iceland (83%), followed by Denmark 78%, Finland (69%), Netherlands (68%) and France (67%).

There were many contrasts, even between close neighbours. Britain was at 54% on the individualised belief scale, whereas Ireland was only at 34%, implying that almost two-thirds of Irish people did not have an individualistic view in 2008.

Spain was at 61%, whereas Italy was only at 24%, a truly remarkable difference between two counties often put in the same box!

The Czech Republic was 52% 'individualised' while Slovakia was only 36%, notwithstanding that they were part of a single state for many years. Germany was only at 52% on the individualism scale, while its neighbours Denmark and Netherlands, as mentioned already, were at 78%, and 68% respectively.

It is clear that newer members of the European Union simply do not share the highly individualistic preferences of some of the older EU states.

It is important that European institutions, including the European Court of Human Rights as well as the EU, take note of what Europeans actually believe, as distinct from what the people administering these institutions personally believe themselves, or decide that Europeans believe.

European Courts can only be used to impose 'European norms' when we have first debated, in a genuinely European electoral process, what those norms are and should be in future.

We do not have such a Europe-wide process at the moment. The values and questions that inform the work of the European Court of Human Rights are not debated in any Europe-wide election, in the same way that the values and questions that inform the judgement of the US Supreme court are debated in US Federal elections.

Judges and regulators need democratic guidance, and we need a Europe-wide venue for this. In the absence of that, judges should be cautious in expanding the field of what constitutes a 'European Right'.

THE GROWTH OF SUPPORT FOR POPULIST PARTIES

UNDERSTANDING THE NEED FOR RESPECT AND RECIPROCITY ARE THE KEYS TO THE FUTURE OF THE EUROPEAN UNION

What do the following have in common?

- The Scottish National Party in the UK,
- The National Front in France,
- The UK Independence Party,
- The Tea Party in the USA, and
- The anti-immigrant parties in Sweden, Denmark, and the Netherlands.

The answer is that all these parties want to withdraw from some international commitment or other and reduce the impact of outside influences on their nation, and they are all enjoying growing support among the electorate.

What support for these parties shows is that introverted nationalism is on the rise again. This is a reaction against globalisation by those who have benefitted less from it than others did. For example, the support for Scottish independence in the decaying industrial regions around Glasgow can be interpreted as a protest against the effects of globalisation. The same can be observed in the geographic spread of support for the National Front in France.

It should be noted that all, including the supporters of populist parties, have benefitted from globalisation, through cheaper food, clothes, and communications. But some have benefitted much more than others, and the 'others' are expressing their disgruntlement by voting for these populist parties.

These parties want a repatriation of powers to the national level, and even complete withdrawal from international bodies like the World Trade Organisation (WTO), the European Union, and the European Convention on Human Rights.

People supporting these parties say they do not understand how Brussels works, or how Westminster or Washington works. But do they really understand any better how their local council works? In a sense, they are rebelling against the compromises that are inherent in democratic politics in a world where the barriers between nations are far less than they were forty years ago. This is why I am unconvinced that concession to their demands would actually remove the discontents that lie behind support for these parties.

For example, I am not convinced that an elaborate system of federalism within the UK, or UK withdrawal from the EU, would actually assuage the anger being expressed through UKIP votes. The experience of regional devolution in post-Franco Spain is not completely reassuring.

In Scotland, the younger and the poorer sections of the population were the most alienated, and voted strongly for Scottish independence. This is despite the fact that public spending per head, on which poorer people usually depend more, is already higher in Scotland than it is in England.

Public spending by the UK Exchequer is £10,152 per head in Scotland, as against £8,529 in England. By those figures, complete fiscal independence would certainly worsen the position of poorer Scots.

These votes reflect a sense of not being listened to, of not being respected, rather than a demand for particular constitutional or institutional changes.

Fear of the future
Fear of what may happen in the future drives people in the direction of populist solutions and parties.

States have made health promises and pension promises that will become unaffordable as the elderly population grows. Meanwhile, many private pension schemes are underfunded.

Another pervasive fear is that of redundancy in midlife. In such a circumstance, it is difficult to know what new skills to go for, and it is equally difficult to move to another city to find work after a certain age.

Anti-immigrant sentiment
These fears feed anti-immigrant sentiment.

Immigration disturbs the bucolic image some people have of their ideal national environment, forgetting that if they actually lived in their ideal environment they would probably find it claustrophobic and boring. People want to preserve the countryside, but they do not necessarily want to live in it.

There is also competition for low-skilled jobs, and immigration does drive some wage rates down. But automation and labour-saving devices are devaluing all forms of low skilled work anyway, and are probably more significant drivers of income inequality than immigration.

Inequality in incomes
The increasing inequality in incomes is also a factor in the growing support for populist parties.

Inequality is driven by many factors. Technology replaces low-skilled workers, while increasing the rewards of the higher skilled people who control the technology.

One should not ignore the role celebrity plays in inequality. Celebrity brings disproportionate increases in relative income. Celebrity footballers and celebrity CEOs represent the same phenomenon. A firm's stock price is driven partly by the reputation of its CEO, and that means a well-known CEO can command a higher salary package.

Inequality is also driven by access to financial leverage and assets that can be used for leverage. Thus high financial sector incomes evoke particular concern.

These are all issues that need to be dealt with by national governments through the tax system. They should not be used to justify turning away from the EU, open trade, or the benefits that globalisation has brought.

The meaning of national identity
We are not going back to a world of empires in which Europeans, or people of European ancestry, could make up the rules of the game to suit themselves. We can perhaps limit the pace of immigration, but we cannot stop it. So we need to update the civic education of ourselves, and of immigrants to our shores, on questions like:

- What does it mean to be British?
- Can one be British, Scottish and European all at the same time?
- What does it mean to be Irish and European, but of African ancestry?
- What are the values that underlie these statements?

Reciprocity
We also need to work out the practical implications of reciprocity as a principle of international relations. Let me illustrate this by reference to debates now taking place in the UK.

If EU citizens migrating to the UK for work are to have restricted access to state benefits, how might that affect the entitlements of the two million UK citizens living in other EU countries? How might it affect their access to health services?

If the UK wants access to an EU single market to sell its goods and services, does that not mean accepting common EU standards for those goods and services?

In particular, the UK wants a single EU market for services, but services are provided by people, and these people may need to travel to another country to provide those services. This brings us back to the immigration debate.

If Britain wants a veto on certain EU laws rather than have them decided by majority, twenty-seven other countries will also have to get that veto too.

If, as some Conservatives propose, the UK withdraws from the European Convention on Human Rights, what effect will that have on the hard-won agreement on policing in Northern Ireland, which depends on access to the European Court of Human Rights?

Democracy is the key to respect
If the EU is to survive, EU citizens need to be able to can cast a vote to change the men or women at the top in the EU, in the same way that they can change the people in Dáil Éireann, in Westminster, in Birmingham City Council, or in their local tennis club.

It is not that citizens want to get into all the details, but they do want a vote on where the EU is going.

Globalisation has taken key decisions beyond the level of individual states for a long time. That is nothing new. But the time has come to make it more democratic.

Traditionally, the rules governing bodies like the International Telecommunication Union (dating back to 1865) and the International Court of Justice (dating back to 1945) were negotiated in private in the form of inter-state treaties between diplomats, later to be interpreted by judges.

The parliaments of the ratifying states were often only involved at the end of the process, by voting to ratify the treaty or not through a simple *yes* or *no*.

The EU is different.

In the EU, politicians in the commission initiate laws, and politicians in the European Parliament and the Council decide if these laws will come into effect. In this sense, the EU is *more* democratic than virtually all other international organisations in the world – but it's not democratic *enough*.

I believe the direct election of the President of the European Commission by the five hundred million people of the EU, not simply by the twenty-eight heads of EU governments, is needed.

Only in that way will we foster a public opinion in the EU that is well-informed and democratic. That would be the best answer of all to the populists.

Why Europe needs to get its act together
In 1989, at the collapse of the Soviet Union, Gorbachev's advisor Alexander Arbatov said to a western diplomat, 'We have done you the worst of services; we have deprived you of an enemy.'

Since then, the lack of perceived external threat has led to weak economic management in Europe, to an unnecessary war in Iraq, to increasing debt, to weakened military strength, and to the making of insincere promises that could not be fulfilled when the going got tough.

Now, that period is over.

We now see, thanks in part to ill-considered promises of eventual NATO membership to Ukraine and Georgia, that those countries have suffered forceful, pre-emptive annexations of parts of their territory by Russia. The UN Charter and the Helsinki Accords on territorial integrity of states have been abandoned. In Eastern Ukraine we are now witnessing what I recently heard a US general describe as 'a new kind of warfare'.

Meanwhile, the growing strength of China's navy distracts the US from Europe, and European and US interests are further diverging as the US has become more and more self-sufficient in energy, while Europe has not.

And productivity in Europe is lagging. According to the OECD, EU labour productivity is growing at 0.6% per annum, while productivity in the rest of the OECD is growing at 1.2% a year.

Rather than contemplating separatism, Europeans should be thinking about our precarious position in the twenty-first-century world, and uniting to do what we can about it.

The above material was first presented on 5 October 2014 in response to the success of anti-EU parties in opinion polls in a number of countries.

LOOSE TALK FROM FOREIGN MINISTERS

In August 2012, some rather strange things were said by the Foreign Ministers of various EU countries in response to the ongoing Greek financial crisis. Sentiments similar to these were voiced by the German Finance Minister in the past few weeks, and the thinking behind them is never far from the surface of public debate. So what follows still needs to be kept in mind.

The Austrian Foreign Minister is reported as having said recently that, 'We need the possibility to throw someone out of the monetary union.' And the Finnish Foreign Minister allegedly said, 'The breakup of the euro does not mean the end of the EU. It could function better.'

Both men should read economist Anders Aslund's paper 'Why a Breakup of the Euro Area must be Avoided: Lessons from Previous Breakups'. Aslund worked as an advisor to the Russian government during the breakup of the rouble currency union between 1991 and 1994.

The rouble had been the common currency of the former Soviet Union, and in his paper Aslund delves into how the breakup of the rouble zone led to 'monetary pandemonium'. Should the euro go down the same path, Europe could face the same consequences. Aslund's paper is published on the website of the Washington-based Peterson Institute for International Economics.

The first thing to say about what the two Foreign Ministers are advocating is that it is illegal.

A country cannot be expelled from the euro under the existing treaties, and those treaties cannot be amended without the consent of all twenty-eight EU states.

This is no mere legalistic point.

The EU has no police force to enforce the provisions of its treaties on those who have signed up to them. The entire existence of the EU rests on the voluntary acceptance of the rules laid down in the EU treaties by everybody. If that is called into question, as it would be if an attempt was made to put a country out of the euro, the whole basis of the EU itself ceases to have any meaning.

The framework of trust within which business is done in Europe would be undermined. One could no longer rely on EU rules being respected. The rule of the strong would be inaugurated, and business between countries would become impossible.

Aslund says that the result of even one country leaving the currency union would be chaotic.

The first major problem would be that of outstanding interbank balances that would be in the European Central Bank (ECB) payments system. What value do you put on these bank balances once a country leaves the eurozone? The ECB system is automated, and allows for money transfers which are essential to keeping commerce flowing. These balances would probably be owed to countries like Germany, with a trade surplus, by countries that are running trade deficits, like Greece.

If the valuation of these balances was disputed – between the euro and whatever new currency was issued by, for example, Greece – trade would freeze up, because no one would trust one another's payments.

Would the balances be settled in newly appreciated euros or in the newly depreciated currency of the countries departing the euro? If one country departed from the euro, which country would be next?

Everyone would send for their lawyers. The economy and trade could simply come to a stop because no one would trust the value of anybody else's money. There would be huge losses of output and capital, which would affect every country – creditors and debtors alike.

Because there would be so much uncertainty about the value of currencies, and doubt about the value of securities held by banks, there would be a risk of people no longer trusting their money in banks at all.

Since the abolition of the gold standard, all credit, and even money itself, is based simply on confidence and trust.

An attempt to break up a supposedly irreversible currency union would undermine the confidence and trust upon which the entire European economy rests.

It would not be like a devaluation of an existing currency, but would instead be an attack on the entire framework underlying money in Europe.

Anders Aslund does not believe it would be possible for one country, like Greece, to leave the euro without the whole system breaking up.

When the rouble-based monetary union of the old Soviet Union broke up, the newly independent central banks of the newly independent republics tried to give their own countries an advantage over others by loosening the purse strings and printing more of their new currencies.

This led to hyperinflation (rates of inflation of 100% or more) and a dramatic fall of about 52% in living standards across all the former Soviet Republics. Some countries are still recovering from the chaos unleashed by the breakup of that rouble monetary union.

It is important for Northern European countries to remember that creditor republics within the former rouble zone, like Russia, lost just as much as the republics that owed them the money.

According to Aslund, 'The causes of these large output falls were multiple: systemic change, competitive monetary emission leading to hyperinflation, the collapse of the payments system, defaults, exclusion from international finance, trade disruption and wars.'

Similar events occurred in Yugoslavia when its currency union broke up, and also when the Austro–Hungarian Empire currency union broke up after the First World War.

In such a situation, people would not want to accept new local currencies if they had the option of using dollars, or another strong currency, whose value would be more reliable. Money would flow into a few strong currencies and these currencies would appreciate artificially.

This would mean a loss of competitiveness for the countries concerned, which might prompt them to reintroduce exchange and capital controls to prevent the loss of their export markets. That would destroy the EU single market.

The single EU market would also be damaged if other EU countries not in the euro used competitive devaluations to win market shares.

The situation in the EU would probably be worse than in the Soviet case, because eurozone economies are much more complex. Also, as we now have more advanced systems of automated and electronic trading, contagion can now spread even more quickly than it could in the 1990s.

Some argue that Greece could gain from leaving the euro because it could devalue, and thus make its exports more attractive. The devaluation would be like an overnight wage cut of 50%. But there could just as easily be a total loss of confidence, a rush of money out of the country, and hyperinflation.

It is also unclear what export markets Greece could quickly exploit with its new, cheap currency, or how its neighbours would react.

The Austrian and Finnish Foreign Ministers should study a little more economic history before they make more statements.

WHAT SORT OF RELATIONSHIP SHOULD THERE BE BETWEEN THE EU AND THE US

I believe it is time for a new EU approach to transatlantic relations. That new approach can only come about if the EU itself works out, all twenty-eight countries together, what we want for ourselves. We must then identify how we, together, can harness our collective weight to achieve our goals through the transatlantic relationship, or through such other means as we decide.

The transatlantic relationship is a means to an end, not an end in itself. That is how the US sees the transatlantic relationship and it is how the EU should see it too.

The norms for EU foreign policy making are clear and binding. The Lisbon Treaty, in Article 21, obliges the EU to follow a policy based on 'democracy, the rule of law, the universality and indivisibility of human rights … respect for human dignity … and respect for the UN charter and international law'.

The EU is a treaty-based organisation, so while EU foreign and security policy is not reviewable by the European Court of Justice (ECJ), it has to be consistent with these words in Article 21 of the treaty, and these treaty obligations supercede other considerations, including the preferences of individual member states.

The treaty also obliges the European Council, in Article 22, to identify 'the strategic interests and objectives' of the union. This means that the European Council is obliged by the treaty to work out, among its twenty-eight members, what the strategic interests and objectives of the European Union as a whole are in regard to issues like:

- Military action in Afghanistan,
- The nature and dimensions of a Palestinian state,
- A fair regime to govern the non-proliferation and eventual elimination of nuclear weapons, and
- Security and energy relations with Russia.

I believe that the necessary new approach to transatlantic relations can only come about after, not before, European countries have worked out between themselves robust common agreements or understandings on these strategic issues.

This will not be an easy task. Some of these issues have yet to be discussed in a profound way in the European Council. But that is the task imposed on the Council by the treaty. It seems to me that the EU treaties have increasingly imposed an unrealistically large range of responsibilities on the European Council. Previously the European Commission might have done this sort of work, but the twenty-eight governments have wanted to take back control – hence the progressive shift in power from a body of full-time Europeans (the Commission) to a body of part-timers (the European Council). Remember that the council consists of the twenty-eight heads of government, who only meet four times a year. These men and women have full-time jobs at home, and are often managing complex domestic coalition governments. This does not allow them the time to do the sort of strategic thinking that the EU treaties formally require them to do. The more the EU enlarges, the bigger the number of people at the Council table and the more difficult it becomes to form a collective view. This explains why the initiative in European affairs is increasingly in the hands of one or two countries, notably Germany. It is as much a consequence of poor constitutional design as of economic power.

In short, the work on EU foreign policy must first be done in Europe, not in Washington, Beijing or Moscow. This is not easy. The EU treaties on foreign policy issues have to be settled by unanimous agreement among the twenty-eight members. The EU frequently finds itself going to meetings with other nations and such without a settled policy, or with policies so general that they are not of much operational use.

The EU used to have only six members; now it has twenty-eight. The more members one has, the more difficult it becomes to achieve unanimity. That is an unavoidable fact.

But it is in recognition of the difficulty of reaching unanimity that the Lisbon Treaty has introduced new arrangements, and given the Union new full-time leadership of a kind that could not be provided by presidencies that rotated every six months.

Having represented the European Union for five years in Washington, I have concluded that the United States would welcome a hard-headed relationship with the European Union.

I believe the United States understands that it will disagree with the European Union from time to time. It may not place the same emphasis as we do on some of the norms we are obliged to follow by Article 21 of our treaty. Inevitably, US interests and EU interests will also diverge. When this happens, I believe the United States will welcome an honest debate followed by a realistic compromise.

In contrast, I do not believe that the United States is particularly interested in a relationship with the EU that is based on drafting long declarations or on launching new processes and institutions. That consumes a lot of bureaucratic time, but does not deliver much that is concrete.

Nor is the United States impressed by EU member states competing with one another to show which of them has the more special relationship with it – who can get the earliest meeting with new US office holders, and who gets the longest meetings in the White House. When President Obama first came to office in 2009, there was a rush of different leaders of the European Union vying to be first, or the one to have the longest, meeting with the new President in the White House. Little thought seems to have been given to how a competitive scramble like this made the European Union appear to the new administration. Perhaps partly because of this, the new administration appeared to me, as EU Ambassador in Washington at the time, to give less attention to the value of the EU as a partner than had the outgoing administration in its last years. Looking to the next administration that will come to office in the US in early 2017, it is important that the EU decide collectively how it will present itself to the administration in its first months, regardless of whether it is a Democratic or a Republican administration.

THE FUTURE OF THE EUROPEAN UNION
— AN IRISH PERSPECTIVE

The euro has helped keep inflation low. Inflation in Germany has been lower in the twelve years since it joined the euro than it was in the twelve preceding years. The euro has created a zone of exchange rate stability, which is very helpful for exports. The usage of the euro in a large number of countries has saved travellers cost and inconvenience, facilitated trade within the eurozone, and brought seigniorage revenues to the eurozone's central banks.

It has increased the availability of credit to households and businesses. Unfortunately this additional credit has not always been prudently used, but the availability of extra credit was beneficial. The euro was at all times a pragmatic project, where one learned by trial and error how best to achieve the ultimate goal.

Some problems were not foreseen, others were not addressed as soon as they might have been, but European Union leaders have, sometimes unduly late in the day, been able to find solutions.

I will deal with some of these problems as I go along, including:

- The narrow focus, and ineffectiveness, of the Stability and Growth Pact,
- The failure of the European Central Bank to use its very explicit Article 14 powers to rein in member state central banks in countries where credit bubbles were developing, and
- The failure, so far at least, to come up with a credible overall plan to recapitalise Europe's banks.

Overall, the thirty-year process leading towards economic and monetary union has brought great benefits to Europe. To understand that, one has only to contemplate what Europe would have been like in the last thirty years if there had been a series of competitive devaluations of national currencies. If that had happened, the common market itself might not have survived. That counterfactual is ignored by many of those who criticise the design of the eurozone.

The goal of economic and monetary union has been part of the European agenda from the immediate post-war period.

When the European Federalists met in Montreux in 1947, they spoke of the need to regulate currencies and capital movements at European level. They recognised that devaluations and protectionism in the inter-war period had aggravated the Depression and contributed to the tensions that led to the Second World War.

When the OEEC, the forerunner of the OECD, was founded in 1948 to help ensure that Marshall Aid was spent effectively, its mandate spoke of the need to avoid financial disequilibrium in Europe, and of the possibility of setting up a European Customs Union.

Nine years later, the Treaty of Rome was agreed between six countries and established the European Common Market. It set the goals of

- Ever closer union among the peoples of Europe,
- Strengthening the unity of member nations' economies, and
- Progressively approximating their economic policies.

The goal of the Treaty of Rome was never a simple free-trade area. It was always more than that. It was an economic union. I fear this was never fully understood or accepted in the United Kingdom.

The first serious outline of a plan for a single currency for Europe was considered at a summit of the leaders of the six Common Market countries in the Hague in 1969. They commissioned a study on economic and monetary union, and a single European currency, from a group chaired by the then Luxembourg Prime Minister, Pierre Werner.

Pierre Werner's report was presented in 1971, before either Britain or Ireland joined the Common Market. However, this report alerted both intending members to the direction in which the EEC was heading. If they did not accept that direction and what it entailed, then they were free not to join at all.

The Werner Report envisaged proceeding towards issuing a European currency in three stages. The first stage would involve free movement of capital between intending members. The second would involve a system of coordination between the central banks of intending members, and the final stage involved fixing exchange rates and issuing a single currency.

The Werner Report was quite specific in saying that economic and monetary union would mean EU involvement in domestic economic policy making. The report, issued in 1971, stated: 'To facilitate the harmonisation of budget policies, searching comparisons will be made of the budgets of the Member States from both quantitative and qualitative points of view. From the quantitative point of view the comparison will embrace the total of the public budgets, including local authorities and social security.'

It was thus clear that EU scrutiny would extend beyond narrow public finance, to include impacts on the broader economy.

It also said: 'It will be necessary to evaluate the whole of the fiscal pressure and the weight of public expenditure in the different countries of the Community and the effects that public receipts and expenditure have on global internal demand and on monetary stability. It will also be necessary to devise a method of calculation enabling an assessment to be made of the impulses that the whole of the public budgets impart to the economy.'

The next big step was the Single European Act of 1986. It sought to introduce majority voting on a range of matters so as to remove barriers to intra-EU trade in goods and services. It also made economic and monetary union an explicit goal in the EU treaties.

To help countries prepare for the extra competition they would face in an economic union, an EU Regional Fund was introduced. Both Ireland and Britain accepted these funds, and in agreeing to the Single European Act, accepted the purpose for which these funds were to be disbursed – namely preparation for economic and monetary union. The UK had a Conservative government, led by Margaret Thatcher, at the time.

In 1989, a second report was prepared with the goal of reviving the project for economic and monetary union. This time the report was prepared by a group chaired by Commission President, Jacques Delors, and on which Ireland was represented by Maurice Doyle, Governor of the Irish Central Bank, and the United Kingdom by Robin Leigh Pemberton, Governor of the Bank of England.

The Delors Report was even more specific than the Werner Report was in envisaging the dangers that inconsistent economic policies within the single currency area could give rise to.

It warned: 'Monetary union without a sufficient degree of convergence of economic policies is unlikely to be durable and could be damaging to the Community. Parallel advancement in economic and monetary integration would be indispensable in order to avoid imbalances.'

It went on to predict exactly what went wrong in Ireland's case. Recalling that financial markets are very bad at predicting crises, and go on lending long after they should have stopped, it said:

'Experience suggests that market perceptions do not necessarily provide strong and compelling signals and that access to a large capital market may for some time even facilitate the financing of economic imbalances. Market forces might either be too slow and weak or too sudden and disruptive. Hence countries would have to accept that sharing a common market and a single currency area imposed policy constraints.'

Unfortunately the Delors Report was all too prescient. Markets, and their handmaidens, the rating agencies, were initially 'too weak and slow' in penalising the build up of excessive borrowing and lending in parts of the eurozone from 2000 on, and then, when they did eventually recognise the problem, they were 'sudden and disruptive' in their response – exactly as Delors predicted.

The next important step in the process of economic integration was the negotiation of the Maastricht Treaty in 1992, which set a precise timetable for the actual achievement of economic and monetary union. It followed the three-stage model recommended by Werner.

Free capital movements came first, in 1990, and restrictions on capital movements were explicitly forbidden in the Maastricht Treaty. The full implications of this were seemingly not envisaged at the time.

It created the conditions in which banks in EU countries could borrow freely from one another across borders.

At retail level, Europe still had national banking systems, supervised by national regulators. But, at wholesale level, free movement of capital meant that the European Union gradually developed a single European banking reality. Banks all over the EU were seeking the highest returns wherever they could find it, increasingly lending to one another, dependent on one another, and vulnerable to one another. The failure to recognise the implications of this is something for which responsibility is widely shared.

The logic of that development should have been a common European Banking policy, with tight supervision from the centre, especially in those parts of the Union where the common interest rate was inappropriately low for local conditions.

The Maastricht Treaty gave the independent European Central Bank a responsibility to 'keep under review' the monetary policies of member states, a right to 'deliver opinions' and to keep capital movements under review.

Furthermore, Article 14 of the statute of the European System of Central Banks says clearly that 'the national central banks are an integral part of the European System of Central Banks and shall act in accordance with the guidelines and instructions of the ECB'.

One must ask then, what use did the ECB make of Article 14 when it saw the disproportionate increase in the size of the banking sector in countries like Ireland and Spain from 2000 on? Did it even consider using that article? If not, why not?

The European Commission has recently claimed that it 'repeatedly signalled downside fiscal and macroeconomic risks related to the property boom in Ireland' from 'as early as 2000'.

If that is so, and given that the ECB had the power under Article 14 of its statute to issue instructions to the Irish Central Bank, one has to ask whether the ECB was listening to what the Commission was saying at all.

If the central bank of a country was allowing its banking sector to grow to 300% of its GDP, surely the ECB should have seen the dangers in that and used its powers?

As a member of the Executive Board of the ECB, Lorenzo Bini Smaghi himself said in Paris, 'It is no surprise that most of the countries with the largest deficits and the largest increases in debt after the crisis have been those in which the financial sector played an increasing role.'

'No surprise,' he said. The financial sector in Ireland and Spain grew disproportionately. That is a fact. Given its overall responsibility for financial stability, should the ECB really have been so surprised by what followed?

From 2000 on, banks from Britain, Germany, Belgium, France, other EU countries, and even American banks, lent irresponsibly to the Irish banks in the hope that they too could profit from the Irish construction bubble.

They did this notwithstanding the fact that they had lots of information available to them about spiralling house prices in Ireland. These lenders were each supervised by their home central banks, and by the ECB, who had the same information available to them too, and who seemingly raised no objection to this lending. Those authorities share responsibility with the Irish Central Bank, but have been less than forthcoming in accepting that.

Of course, primary responsibility for this rests with the Irish authorities who did not supervise the Irish banks properly. There were, however, major failures of prudential supervision at wider European level too, in other central banks, and in the ECB.

Irish taxpayers, in taking the private liabilities of the Irish banks to other European banks in 2008, are now helping to stabilise the situation of European banks, and of the European banking system.

There is a tendency in some quarters to glide over that fact, and to present it as a purely Irish problem with purely Irish responsibility. While that story may be comforting to some audiences, it is not the whole story, and blinds us to lessons that need to be learned at a wider European level.

In the Greek case, it is slightly different. There the excessive borrowing was by the Greek government as well as by the Greek banks. Considering it was government borrowing, it could be argued that there is a greater Greek taxpayer responsibility. But even in the Greek case there is a shared responsibility. Nobody forced the banks in other countries to lend as they did to the Greek government or to Greek banks. It is argued by some that the Greek government has taken on unsustainable debts, partly to make sure banks in other countries were repaid and their governments did not have to rescue them.

There is an issue of fairness here that will ultimately have to be faced. It would be wrong to give Greece a debt write off before it has tackled the underlying causes of its problems, such as poor tax collection, inefficient legal systems, corruption, overstaffing of the civil service, bloated state enterprises, and unduly early retirement. Even when all these problems are tackled, and a Greek export economy is re-established, there is a real possibility that debt levels of the Greek government will remain too high, and that Greece may not be able to roll over these debts when they fall due. So, in order to give Greece an incentive for reform action now, it might be a good idea for the European Union, with the IMF, to offer the possibility of a European Debt Conference in 2022 (when Greece has particularly big repayments to make) on the basis that relief would be considered at that stage, but only if all reform commitments had been honoured in the meantime.

One has to admit that when we came, at the Dublin EU Summit in 1996, to set up the Stability and Growth Pact to give effect to the Maastricht Treaty, we again made the mistake of focusing exclusively on government finances. We neglected the possibility that trouble could be caused by private sector excesses, and that to avoid that we needed tougher transnational European banking supervision.

As I have said, this omission subsequently facilitated pro-cyclical monetary expansion in some countries, like Ireland and Spain.

Interest rates that were suitable to Germany, as it went through the difficult post-reunification phase, were too low for Ireland and Spain. When local Irish and Spanish inflation was taken into account, they were actually negative. In a sense, Irish and Spanish borrowers were being subsidised to borrow, and the ECB knew this. This subsidy, through interest rates, was unfortunately supplemented by domestic tax reliefs for certain types of borrowing. When interest rates are negative, you create an incentive for the creation of pro-cyclical bubbles in the economy.

In putting that right, we must not overreact in the opposite direction.

When at the bottom of a market, insisting in marking all bank assets to the price they could realise if sold immediately, and into a market in which nobody can afford to buy them, would aggravate an already difficult situation. It would destroy value and make no economic sense.

On 25 March, EU leaders will come together to agree a new treaty-based fund to help countries that get into difficulty. This will subsequently be adopted as the Fiscal Compact Treaty, and will be underpinned by a competitiveness pact.

The latest draft of the competitiveness pact has been prepared by President Van Rompuy of the European Council and President Barroso of the European Commission. It focuses on measures to be taken by member states in their own field of competence. In this respect it is an elaboration of the so-called Lisbon Strategy, but it contains a somewhat more rigorous invigilation of what states do, and do not do, in respect of the commitments they make under the pact.

The focus is on:

- Reducing labour costs in countries with competitiveness problems,
- Decentralising wage bargaining,
- Opening up professions and energy networks to competition,
- Less expensive legal systems,
- Raising the retirement age,
- Introducing a constitutional or other legal limit on government borrowing, and
- Having a single consolidated base for corporation tax.

Most of these proposals are good and sensible. The European Commission will have an important role in monitoring all this, and in proposing changes in policy when member states depart from the pact.

On the suggestion of a common, consolidated tax base, Ernst & Young have estimated that a common consolidated tax base would add a net 13% to the tax compliance costs of Irish firms. Another study suggests that big countries with big markets would collect more tax under it, while smaller peripheral countries would collect less, thereby worsening their relative debt repayment position.

I am also not sure that it is sufficient to rely on heads of government policing one another to ensure that commitments are delivered. A study for the European Parliament showed that the Country Specific Recommendations, approved by the heads of governments at summits in 2011, 2012, and 2013, had a very poor record of implementation. The rate of implementation ranged from a high of 30% to a low of 15%. And these are recommendations that heads of governments are making to their *own* governments.

While small countries may submit to peer pressure from big countries, the process rarely works in reverse, when bigger countries are the ones needing to respond. The experience of trying to apply the Stability and Growth Pact to Germany and France in 2004 is a case in point. That part of the Van Rompuy/Barroso proposal must be strengthened if it is to be credible. Again, this concern has proven to be well-founded, with France getting greater leniency after its failure to achieve deficit targets than was extended to smaller countries.

The idea of a constitutional debt brake will bring lawyers into the centre of fiscal policy making. I am not convinced that this will improve matters. It would be useful to study the history of a similar effort in the United States, the Gramm–Rudman law. The debt brake could become a political football. It needs to be very carefully designed, leaving room to deal with genuine emergencies. This aspect of the Fiscal Compact Treaty has yet to be put to the test.

That said, it is absolutely right that we focus on getting public debt under control. The US Congressional Budget Office predicts that, on present trends, US Federal debt service will rise from 10% of US revenues today, to 58% by 2040. Our present difficulties, and the prospective cost of an ageing population, put most European governments on a similar trajectory.

The real problem in making sure these proposals are

implemented is designing penalties for errant behaviour which goes beyond mere peer pressure.

Under the present rules, we say we will impose fines on countries that exceed the deficit limits (but interestingly, not the debt limits). These rules have not worked.

I have two concerns here.

Firstly, in some countries, like Ireland, government deficits were not the primary problem; the expansion of private sector credit was, and there were, and are, no penalties for that. Nor are any proposed.

Secondly, imposing fines on countries that already cannot pay their way because of their deficit is like trying to draw blood from a stone. Using fines, or the threat of fines, to get to countries that are already in financial difficulty is perverse insofar as the fine actually adds to their difficulty. Consideration should be given to devising carrots, as well as sticks, to encourage countries to adhere to debt and deficit targets, and to implement EU-recommended structural reforms to increase the growth potential of their economy. One such carrot might be the right to issue Eurobonds, which would carry a guarantee of repayment backed by all the Eurozone governments, and not just that of the issuing government. Conditions for the issue of Eurobonds, and of continuing mutual guarantee, could include having debt and deficit levels in line with Commission recommendations for two years, and fully implementing structural reforms in the same period. While interest rates on sovereign debt are low now, this may not always be so and such a facility could then become attractive.

We must design a new system which will ensure that the markets do their job properly and in good time, and are not allowed to be 'too slow and too weak' in reacting to problems in particular countries, as the Delors Report feared they would be. The best way may be for the supervisory authorities to rub the markets' noses in problems they might otherwise ignore until it is too late. I suggest that this could be achieved if the European Council decided that the Commission and the ECB should adopt a policy of formally and regularly briefing the rating agencies and all the political parties in all member states with their candid assessment of emerging problems in competitiveness, credit growth, and public finance imbalances in each member state.

Thus, rather than rely on cumbersome bureaucratic procedures in the European institutions to eventually pressure countries to put problems right, more reliance would be placed on competitive markets – financial and political – to deliver the necessary policy changes. I believe this would be much more effective than peer pressure at closed-door meetings in Brussels.

EU-recommended structural reforms have offered no proposals on that subject. They seem to assume that the problem is solved, and that a push on competitiveness is all that is needed. I disagree.

The Union must tackle the problem of recapitalising Europe's banking system and show how that can be done over a reasonable time frame.

I accept that there will be no transfer union within the eurozone. The political conditions for it do not exist.

However, a proposal to relaunch Europe's banking system would have far more support than a transfer union. George Soros recently wrote that the EU's emergency funds should all be used to recapitalise Europe's banks. If that is not to be done, there must be an alternative.

Considerable progress has been made in this matter since these words were written. 130 eurozone banks are now subject to a Single Supervisory Mechanism. However, they do not supervise other banks who still account for 20% of all eurozone bank deposits. A Single Resolution Mechanism, backed by a Single Resolution Fund, has also been set up to close down banks that are a threat to the system. There is a provision for a bail-in whereby stakeholders in a failing bank would have to contribute, but there is worry that these mechanisms will not be able to act quickly enough, and that the Resolution Fund is too small. Too many actors may have to be consulted for speed and confidentiality to be maintained. In a crisis, the markets would test these arrangements very aggressively. An unlimited backstop is needed, but the willingness is not yet there to provide it.

Europe's banking system is three and a half times Europe's GDP, whereas the US banking system is only 80% of the US GDP. Loan to deposit ratios are considerably higher in Europe too. Europe relies very heavily on banks because it has not developed adequate alternative means of raising finance.

It is arguable that Europe's banks are now so interdependent on one another that the problem of recapitalising banks should be a European, rather than a member state, responsibility. It is also arguable that central banking policy has added to problems, rather than mitigated them. The Basel II system that central banks were using until recently was pro-cyclical during the boom. The new rules may prove to be pro-cyclical too, but in the opposite direction. The high capital requirements may artificially restrict credit and slow recovery.

We need to take a European view about the size of banks, the interconnectedness of banks, and the 'too big to fail' problem, as well as a host of other difficult questions. Unless we restore our banking system, confidence will not return, small businesses will not thrive and we will lack the necessary credit to tackle our structural problems.

For example, Europe has only 0.6% of the world's oil reserves, but it consumes 17% of the world's oil production.

A recent paper commissioned by the German Ministry of the Environment suggested that achieving a 30% reduction in Europe's CO_2 emissions by 2030 could add 0.6% to European GDP growth and create 600,000 jobs in renewables, smart grids, insulation, public transport, etc.

This may not work, but necessity is the mother of invention. The industrial revolution started in Britain in the eighteenth century, rather than on the continent, because labour costs were higher in Britain. This gave British eighteenth-century industrialists the incentive to adopt labour-saving machinery.

Perhaps the high cost of imported oil and gas will now give Europe the necessary incentive to adopt radical energy-saving technologies. But that cannot happen unless we have a properly functioning banking system to lend to the entrepreneurs making the breakthroughs.

To conclude, the problems the European Union faces today are challenging not only politically, but intellectually. But they are problems that the rest of the world will have to face sooner or later. Europeans are the world's pioneers of economic integration.

Those who founded the European Union had enormous intellectual self-confidence. That self-confidence must be rediscovered. There must be a coming together of minds in place of the institutional rivalry that sometimes characterises European Union politics. Lessons must be learned and problems must be confronted honestly, but once that is done, we must work together to find practical and imaginative solutions.

To sustain an economic and monetary union in the long run, we need to create a true European *demos*, and a European patriotism. That is needed to make the occasional transfers of funds from one part of the union to another politically acceptable, and that will be needed if a single currency is to work in the long term.

We have not created a European *demos*, nor have we created a common European patriotism, as has unfortunately become all too obvious.

The above material is based on a lecture I gave in the APCO 'Worldwide Perspectives on Europe' series of lectures, at the London School of Economics on 7 March 2011.

WHAT DOES BRITAIN WANT FROM AN EU RENEGOTIATION, AND WHAT TERMS WOULD IT GET IF IT LEFT?

In December 2013, I took part in an exercise in London organised by the think tank, Open Europe.

It first examined the issues that might arise in a possible renegotiation of the United Kingdom's terms of membership of the European Union. (The exercise was conducted on the basis that the participants played a role. The role in which I was cast was that of the European Commission.)

It then went on to look at the terms the UK might get if, in a referendum, voters in the UK decided to withdraw from the EU.

This referendum is inevitable. Referenda are unpredictable, and frequently decided on grounds that are not central to the issue actually put before the people.

The British Prime Minister, David Cameron, has raised the question of a British renegotiation of its membership terms at an EU Summit, but to date there is no published list of UK negotiating goals.

The only country in the EU where the potential issues of a UK renegotiation or withdrawal are being debated at all is in the UK itself. That debate is narrowly focused on UK concerns, and takes little account of the effect on the twenty-seven other member states of the EU, including Ireland, of the various UK renegotiation/withdrawal scenarios.

Other EU leaders have taken a vow of silence on the internal UK debate, even though it is one in which their own electorates have a vital interest.

Understandably, they do not want to aggravate UK public

opinion, which might resent 'foreign' intervention in what would be construed – entirely inaccurately – as a purely domestic UK matter.

The downside of this approach is that UK public and media opinion may develop unrealistic expectations of the terms it could achieve in a renegotiation, leading to disappointment, and a consequent increase in support for outright withdrawal.

David Cameron has been deliberately unspecific about the demands the UK will make. Others in his party have been less reticent.

This is what the Mayor of London, Boris Johnson, has had to say: 'If we can knock out social and environmental legislation, if we can knock out the Common Agricultural Policy, if we can repatriate powers over global justice and home affairs, if we can manage migration ourselves, if we can genuinely complete the single market in services, then maybe, maybe we're going to win this argument.'

If these are the expectations senior Conservatives have of what they might achieve in a renegotiation, they might be better off to simply apply to withdraw straight away, and not waste time on renegotiating terms of membership.

There is one issue on which David Cameron's demands are already very explicit and clear – the rights of recent EU immigrants living in the UK. This may, or may not, include Irish immigrants living in Britain, but I expect it could be difficult in EU law for Britain to discriminate in favour of the Irish against other EU nationals.

The Conservative Manifesto could not be clearer on the position of recent immigrants from other EU countries. It says that 'if (EU) jobseekers have not found a job within 6 months, they will be required to leave.'

This seems to be in direct conflict with Article 20 of the EU Treaty which gives EU citizens a right to 'move and reside freely within the territory of (other) member states'.

Furthermore, the Manifesto recalls that the government has already banned housing benefit for EU immigrants, and goes on to say, 'we will insist that EU migrants who want to claim tax credit and child benefit must have lived here for five years.'

This seems in flat contradiction of Article 45 of the EU Treaty which requires 'the abolition of any discrimination based on nationality between workers as regards employment, remuneration, and other conditions of employment'.

Tax credits are a form of negative income tax. If discrimination in respect of tax credits were to be permitted within the EU, it would become impossible to resist applying different income tax rates, or different tax free allowances, to people of different EU nationalities.

In fact, EU countries are already so integrated with one another, that almost anything that the UK is likely to ask for in a renegotiation is already a domestic issue for some or all members.

The UK needs to take account of opinion in other EU states, and of the interests of other EU states. It is not hearing any informed expression of either opinion or interests at the moment.

The consent of a majority of the other EU states will be needed if

- A renegotiation is to be concluded to the satisfaction of the UK (if what the UK is conceded requires a Treaty change, all of the twenty-seven other members will have to unanimously agree), or
- If the UK is to withdraw from the EU, a majority among the other EU states would also be needed to agree the terms of a new EU relationship with the UK, and to allow, for example, continuing privileged access for the UK to the EU Single Market.

Neither of these can be taken for granted.

The first question the UK should ask itself is whether it is in the national interest of the UK that the EU itself remains a viable and confident institution after the various scenarios have been played out.

If a successful EU is deemed to be in Britain's interests, Britain should not make demands of the EU which, if conceded, would damage (or indeed destroy) the EU. This applies whether the UK itself intends to stay in the EU or not.

The precedent of an EU member state getting preferential terms because of a threat withdrawal could corrode mutual confidence among the remaining twenty-seven members. Some UK Conservatives may not be worried about that, but those with whom they will be in negotiation will have to take that into account. Suppose, for example, there is a National Front-led government in France, it will also feel obliged to look for big concessions to France alongside the UK demands. If these are all conceded, the EU will be no more.

One gets the impression that some in the UK do not care about this, others have not thought about it, and others still would actually be happy if the whole process tore the EU apart.

My own sense is that, whether it is a member itself or not, the UK has a vested interest in the EU remaining effective. An effective EU keeps Europe at peace, and it creates a single open market at Britain's doorstep, which is good for British trade. Britain would not sell as much in a Europe that had reverted to twenty-seven different markets with twenty-seven different currencies, different standards, and possibly capital controls and tariff barriers.

An EU that could not make decisions, because it was paralysed by fear about who might follow the UK out the door, would not be good for Britain either.

Furthermore, some of the likely UK renegotiation proposals would undermine the effectiveness and stability of the EU in an even more direct way.

One such proposal is a so-called 'Red Card', whereby a minority of national parliaments could veto an EU law, even though that law

- Had already been passed by majority in both the Council of Ministers, where all states (including the UK) would have had a vote, and
- Has been passed by a majority in the European Parliament, where all states (including the UK) have directly-elected MEPs.

This idea of a Red Card has won support from the British Foreign Secretary and even from some in the Labour Party.

The Fresh Start Group of 100 Conservative MPs has gone

further, and said that an unspecified group of national parliaments should be able to repeal existing EU laws, bypassing the European Parliament and the EU's existing decision-making structures.

This Red Card would paralyse EU decision making, in ways that might not suit the UK itself. It could also be used in turn by others to block the very measures that the UK wants, such as the liberalisation of the services market in the EU.

A provision whereby shifting majorities among national parliaments could bypass the EU's democratic decision-making procedures, and unilaterally repeal previously settled EU laws and agreements, would completely undermine the stability of the EU single market.

It would become an instrument for reopening long settled compromises on which the EU single market is based, and making them subject to populist pressures on an ongoing basis.

Both of these proposals would require a Treaty change, because the role of national parliaments in the EU process is defined in a protocol of the existing treaties, and a protocol has the same legal status as an article in the treaties themselves. To change the protocol in question, every one of the twenty-eight member states and the European Parliament would have to agree.

Another likely UK demand would be to opt out of having the European Court of Justice as the final adjudicator on disputes concerning the meaning of EU agreements regarding the fight against crime. The UK is likely to demand that these issues be adjudicated in national courts instead, which could mean twenty-eight different interpretations, and many new loopholes through which well-advised criminals could evade justice.

If the UK electorate is not satisfied with the terms offered to keep the UK in the EU, and votes that the UK should withdraw from the EU, a second negotiation would start.

The purpose of that negotiation would be to decide the terms on which the UK, outside the EU, would have access to the EU for its people, goods, and services. This second negotiation would have to be concluded within two years.

It would be conducted under Article 50 of the EU Treaty, which requires a qualified majority in the European Council and a majority in the European Parliament to agree on the terms to be granted to a country withdrawing from the EU. It is likely that such terms would include a continuing financial contribution to the EU budget, in return for UK access to the EU single market. That is the precedent.

In the event of no agreement being reached within the two-year deadline (which is in the Treaty and cannot be extended without a Treaty change), the UK would be out of the EU, and automatically subject to restrictions and tariffs on its exports to EU countries of goods and services, as if it had never been an EU member. Customs posts would have to be reintroduced on the border in Ireland and at cross-Channel ports overnight. Given the brinkmanship that is routine in EU negotiations, and the rigidity of the terms of Article 50, this is no mere academic possibility.

Furthermore, if the UK, then outside the EU, wanted to restrict immigration from the EU, it would have to introduce passport controls on the Irish border, a measure that would undermine the work done to promote peace and reconciliation.

These are really serious questions, and it is deeply regrettable that British democracy is debating them in such a superficial manner.

Book Reviews

THE REAL LESSONS OF THE CUBAN MISSILE CRISIS: STILL RELEVANT, BUT PERHAPS IGNORED, FIFTY-ONE YEARS LATER

The Cuban Missile Crisis in American Memory
Sheldon M. Stern (Stanford University Press, 2012)

One of the events that shaped my youth was the Cuban Missile Crisis of October 1962.

Like almost everybody else, I believed that the Soviet plan to locate nuclear armed missiles in Cuba was a direct threat to the United States and that, in facing down that threat, President John F. Kennedy had saved the world (and his own country) from an imminent danger.

'Standing up to the Soviets' was thus seen to be the best and safest policy to secure peace. From that lesson came the US policy that standing one's ground was the right policy to follow, for example in South Vietnam.

The murder of President Kennedy just a year after the Cuban Missile Crisis meant that historians did not question the President's policy on Cuba very rigorously. It also meant that other Presidents, like Johnson and Nixon, were the ones who took the responsibility if bad things resulted from trying to apply the supposed lessons of the Cuban Missile Crisis.

A new book has been published by Stanford Press which calls all this into question. It is called *The Cuban Missile Crisis in American*

Memory by Sheldon M. Stern. This book was reviewed by Benjamin Schwartz in the *Atlantic* magazine, early in 2013.

It makes the case that the Kennedy administration itself had provoked the crisis by deploying Jupiter missiles in Italy and Turkey in 1961, aimed at the Soviet Union. These missiles were not a mere deterrent. They were clearly aggressive in intent, because they were visible, immovable, and above ground.

Thus, they could only be militarily useful in the event of a nuclear first strike by the US against the Soviet Union, because if the Soviets had decided to use nuclear weapons first, they would have made sure to knock these missiles out of commission, in the first seconds of their attack.

The Soviet decision to send missiles to Cuba was a direct response to this deployment of missiles in Turkey and Italy a few months earlier and was an attempt to get Kennedy to understand exactly how the Soviets felt about the missiles in Italy and Turkey.

Many thought that deployment of Soviet missiles in Cuba was a unique new risk to the US, because the countries are so close.

Schwartz says this was not so, and that there was a negligible difference in flight times to the US between intercontinental missiles based in the Soviet Union and missiles to be based in Cuba. Schwartz claims that President Kennedy knew that the proposed Cuban-based missiles did not pose a special new threat, but that he felt he had to be *seen* not to back down in the face of the Soviet move. For that he was apparently prepared to run a real risk of a nuclear war.

Kennedy could have asked the Soviets, at the outset of the crisis, to agree on a mutual decommissioning of missiles, but he did not make that offer at that time.

Eventually that was precisely the deal that did end the crisis. But, according to Schwartz, 'Kennedy threatened to abrogate [the deal] if the Soviets disclosed it'. For domestic US purposes, he wanted the Soviets to appear to have backed down. The lesson here is that politics can get in the way of realistic security policy.

As another Democratic US President seeks to deal with further risks of nuclear proliferation, it is wise to understand and reflect on the real lessons of the Cuban Missile Crisis.

A LONG-FORGOTTEN WAR

∞

Crimea: The Last Crusade,
Orlando Figes (Allen Lane, 2010)

It is not much remembered today, but in the parishes of Whitegate and Aghada in East Cork, where the British Army recruited heavily, almost one third of the male population died in the Crimean War. In fact, almost one-third of the British Army deployed in the Crimea was Irish. It was the earliest example of a truly modern war, fought with new industrial technologies, and with modern communications and modern media hype.

I recently read *Crimea: The Last Crusade* by Orlando Figes. Figes is a specialist in Russian history, and brings a new perspective to a war that is usually remembered from a British point of view.

The origin of the war lay in the Russian Tsar's ambition to increase his influence in the Ottoman Empire, both in general, and in particular in his role as the protector there of Orthodox Christians. He was very sensitive to preference being shown by the Ottoman authorities to Latin Christians (Catholics and Protestants) over the Orthodox, especially in the Holy Land (then Ottoman Palestine). This preference was partly a result of French pressure on the Ottoman authorities, and the Tsar wanted to counteract. In a sense, there was a conflict 150 years ago over rival spheres of influence between different powers, an issue that persists to this day.

While the immediate cause of hostility was a dispute about rights in the Holy Sepulchre Church in Jerusalem, there was a wider fear of Russian expansionism, and of Russian ambitions to create a sphere of influence that would threaten British and French interests in the Middle East.

There are echoes of current controversies in Afghanistan. The Ottomans had only abolished the death penalty for Muslims who converted to Christianity in 1844, and even still, a number of executions took place after that.

Against that background, it is surprising that France and Britain joined Ottoman Turkey in a religiously motivated war against Russia. It illustrates the hostility that exists, to this day, between Orthodox and Latin Christians – something that is currently under the surface of modern politics in the Balkans.

The immediate reason for Britain and France joining Turkey in a war against Russia was Russian occupation of Ottoman provinces in present-day Romania and Moldova. This occupation was not intended to be permanent, but was a gambit to obtain other concessions from the Ottomans, notably better rights for Orthodox Christians than those available to Latin Christians.

Instead of conceding to Russian demands, the Turks declared war on Russia in late 1853. The Russians then destroyed the Turkish fleet, which was portrayed as a war crime in the British and French media. Russian occupation of Ottoman territory was not presented in the same light.

France and Britain declared war on Russia in March 1854. They decided to attack Russia in the Crimea, a territory Russia had taken from Turkey in the previous century. Lord Aberdeen, the British Prime Minister, hoped to roll back Russian power, forcing it to hand Finland back to Sweden, and to give the Crimea, Circassia and Georgia back to the Ottomans.

The French were better prepared for the war than the British. French troops had winter supplies, but the British did not. The French also had better medical supports and systems for feeding their soldiers in the field. Both the French and British had much better rifles than the Russians, but the Russians had better anaesthetics which enabled them to perform battlefield surgery more quickly and to save more lives.

Although, technically speaking, the Russians lost the war when it ended in 1856, the Allies did not achieve their war aims.

The religious and political bitterness engendered by the war led to atrocities when it was over. Muslim Circassians and Tatars, suspected of collaboration with the Allies, were driven out of their homeland by the Russians. 20,000 Maronite Christians were massacred in Ottoman-controlled Lebanon, and there were attacks on Christians in Nablus and Gaza. Christian Armenians then emigrated from Ottoman territory to Russia because they feared a similar fate.

The fall of Communism has brought many of the old antagonisms that were on display during the Crimean war and in its aftermath back to the forefront of modern politics. That relevance to current tension in Crimea, Georgia, Lebanon and Armenia is what made this book so interesting.

HOW CAN DEMOCRACY BE RECONCILED WITH GLOBALISATION? CAN OUR NEEDS AS INVESTORS, CONSUMERS AND CITIZENS BE RECONCILED?

Supercapitalism: The Transformation of Business, Democracy and Everyday Life,
Robert B. Reich (Vintage, 2008)

In his book, *Supercapitalism: The Transformation of Business, Democracy and Everyday Life*, Robert Reich argues that technologies that were developed to fight the Cold War – computers, software, telecommunications and super-light alloys – along with containerisation and cheap transport, opened up previously closed markets to global competition.

This has meant that the effective control of economics is no longer exercised by national governments, who are accountable to national electorates. Instead, control is now exercised at global level, where competitive forces are much stronger than democratic impulses. The forms of democracy remain, but the substance has moved elsewhere.

Because goods and services can be sourced anywhere in the world, competition between firms is now more intense than at any time in history. As Reich sees it, competition has drowned out other concerns. Human needs, such as the need for job security, now take second place in many firms to achieving the lowest possible consumer price index and the highest possible returns for investors.

In practice, the situation is not as stark as Reich says. Even in the US, where the law gives firms great freedom to hire and fire, firms recognise it is in their commercial interest to make their staff feel secure in their jobs, so as to maximise their productivity and commitment to the firm. As jobs become more specialised, firms want to avoid the cost of retraining new people to replace someone who has left because they felt insecure in their job. 'Employee engagement' is a key metric of success for management.

Reich argues that all of us have three roles: as a citizen, as a consumer, and as an investor. Many people exercise their 'investor' role indirectly, through pensions and insurance policies to which they contribute. Global competition has put our demands as consumers and investors far ahead of our needs as citizens. As Reich sees it, firms compete for markets and for shareholders in a much more intense way than before, because better communications, freedom of capital movement, and open markets have meant that they can no longer afford the high wages and the philanthropic approach possible before the arrival of globalisation.

As consumers or investors, we are not always aware that the much lower prices we are getting in the shop, or the higher return we were getting in our pension fund, has come (to some degree) at the expense of our own job security and our own environment.

Reich argues that it is futile to expect corporations to behave differently. Under law, their obligation is to maximise the return to their shareholders. It is a waste of time asking corporations to be good citizens. Only people can be citizens, he argues. This is an overstatement. To retain valuable employees, firms have to show that they are doing socially valuable things, whether in their main business or as part of corporate social responsibility programmes.

Reich contrasted all of this with what he called the 'Not Quite Golden Age' – between 1945 and 1970 – when competition was less intense and companies had resources to spare to act as good citizens and to pay good wages to those lucky enough to have a job.

That was then possible because the predominant industrial system was one of mass production, and the costs of setting up for mass production were so large that established firms had a protected market in which they could overcharge consumers. That ability to overcharge allowed them to be philanthropic and/or to pay higher wages.

They did not have to pay much attention to shareholders either, because national exchange and capital controls meant that investors had limited choices about where to put their money. This gave their trade unions greater bargaining power, so wages and job security were better. But the downside of all this was a lower overall level of employment and economic activity. It is also worth saying that in the 'Not Quite Golden Age', while wages may have been relatively higher than they are today, the jobs were held mainly by men; women worked to a greater extent in unpaid work in the home. The new era of globalisation has coincided with a big increase in the paid workforce, with far more women in paid employment, and the resultant local competition for jobs may have contributed to downward pressure on wages. There has been a trade-off between more jobs and more pay.

Reich said this 'Not Quite Golden Age' will never come back. The forces driving globalisation are physical and technological, and they cannot be reversed by political action in one country, unless that country seals itself off from the rest of the world, like North Korea. Even East Germany had to take down its wall.

Unfortunately Reich puts forward few remedies to the problems he has analysed so well. He suggests a transfer tax on shares, a law to briefly postpone redundancies, and greater trade union rights. But if one country tried to put these measures into force on its own, even a big country like France, it would probably lose investors and market share, and then have to reverse these measures under pressure from market forces.

This is the weakness of much modern socialist and social democratic thinking. It offers solutions that would have worked in the 'Not Quite Golden Age', but that are impractical now, because they fail to recognise the changes wrought in the global economy by globalisation since 1970.

Just as climate change can only be tackled by democratically agreed global agreements, the excesses of global competition can only be managed at global level too. The G20, not national capitals, is where the action is. But the G20 is not democratically elected, whereas national governments are. We need to imagine a new politics of globalisation, and create official fora in which voters have a sense that they can impact the work of bodies like the G20, the OECD, and the World Trade Organisation. The European Parliament, one of the world's few directly elected supranational parliaments, is a model that should be followed more widely. Why not have a directly elected parliament to oversee the work of the OECD?

HOW WILL THE TWENTY-FIRST CENTURY TURN OUT?

The Next 100 Years: A Forecast for the 21st Century,
George Friedman (Anchor, 2009)

George Friedman is the founder of Stratfor, a Texas-based strategic intelligence consultancy, which advises many major US corporations. Although described as a conservative Republican, his views would mirror those of many foreign policy realists, Democratic and Republican alike.

He assumes that military and economic power will determine the future. As he puts it, 'anger does not make history, power does'.

Looking back at his book six years later, it appears to have been prescient in many respects.

He argued that the United States would remain the dominant global power for the rest of the twenty-first century thanks to its huge natural resources of coal and oil, its geographic immunity from attack in North America, and its control of space and the world's seas.

Just as Britain's strategic goal, as an island nation and a naval power, was to prevent Europe's unification under a one power coalition, America will pursue a similar policy on the Eurasian land mass. It will not want any one coalition – be it of Russia, China, Turkey or Japan – to dominate that land mass.

He was critical of the way American politicians sometimes approached foreign policy. Because America is so powerful, it has a much bigger margin of error than other smaller or less powerful countries, and it sometimes overuses that luxury. He said America is 'adolescent in its simplification of issues, and in its use of power'. In general, I do not think President Obama can be accused of this, but some of his Republican critics can.

Most significantly, in light of current events, Friedman argued that Russia, following the eastward expansion of NATO to within one hundred miles of St Petersburg, was 'in an untenable political position' and 'unless it exerts itself to create a sphere of influence, it could itself fragment'. This is a credible explanation of Putin's present actions in Georgia and Ukraine.

He saw both China and Japan as vulnerable, because they are export economies and rely on the all-powerful US Navy to keep sea lanes open for their exports of goods and their imports of raw material. Since 2009, China has spent heavily on its navy, so this prediction may be overturned.

Friedman said that the European Union was a schizophrenic entity, in that its 'primary purpose is the creation of an integrated economy, while leaving sovereignty in the hands of individual nations'. The current economic crisis is putting this proposition to the test, and one hopes Friedman will be proved wrong. But he has a point. EU states often set ambitious common objectives for themselves, but fail to match them with the necessary central authority.

He argued that there is a divergence of interest between Germany and others who will want easy relations with Russia, and more easterly EU members, fearful of being sucked back into Russia's sphere of influence. Chancellor Merkel does seem to be confronting this dilemma, if reluctantly.

Surprisingly, Friedman did not see China becoming a great power. This was because of what he saw as its inefficient allocation of capital, its corruption, its profitless exports and its unhealthy reliance on US consumers to buy its goods. Its one-child policy will also mean that it will soon be an ageing society. It appears that the current Chinese leadership is confronting these challenges, but reorienting its entire economy will be a very difficult process.

Surprisingly, Friedman saw Japan emerging as the major Asian power, notwithstanding its lack of resources and its very elderly population. I believe this is incredible. An elderly country cannot be a powerful country. He ignored India completely. I believe this analysis of the long-term balance of power in Asia to be quite unconvincing.

He saw Turkey emerging as the major power across all the former Ottoman lands from North Africa to Central Asia. Here his predictions are more robust in light of subsequent events. He argued that Islamic fundamentalism will run out of steam because its real target, the liberation of women, is irreversible. Since he wrote his book, Islamic fundamentalism has actually increased in strength, but he is probably right in the long term.

Friedman speculated about the likely conflicts of the twenty-first century – including its wars. He believed the wars will be conducted by unmanned aircraft using high-precision weaponry guided from space. They will be backed up by small numbers of highly equipped infantry. The aim will be to destroy the electricity generation capacity and close sea lanes of the enemy. There will be modest casualties. Wars, he believed, would be limited and would end with negotiated treaties. Pursuit of unconditional surrender would be off the agenda because nuclear weapons would make it too dangerous. All this is true of wars between the big nuclear powers, but are hardly true of what we have been seeing in Ukraine, Syria, Iraq and parts of Africa.

Although some of Friedman's speculations had a touch of science fiction about them, its basic assumptions about the realities of military power and its reach are credible and sobering, especially for those who might think that neutrality would protect a country from military conflicts.

LAND, RELIGION, SECULARISM AND POWER POLITICS:
THE STORY OF MEXICO

Mexico, Biography of Power: A History of Modern Mexico 1810–1996,
Enrique Krauze (Harper Perennial, 1998)

Enrique Krauze's *Mexico, Biography of Power* approaches the history of the country through the biographies of strong leaders who dominated the country for the last two hundred years. It introduces readers to the revolutionary priest Miguel Hidalgo, the theatrical General Santa Anna, the French-backed would-be Habsburg Emperor of Mexico Maximilian, the pure-blooded native Mexican Benito Juarez, and the moderniser who would not willingly give up power, Porfirio Diaz.

After the fall of Diaz came the Revolution of 1910, which ushered in almost twenty years of civil war, first between the revolutionaries themselves, and then between the Revolution and Catholic guerrillas, the 'Cristeros', who objected to the restrictions the revolution was placing on the work of the church.

The book deals with the formation of the Partido Revolucionario Institucional (PRI), the party that dominated Mexican politics for most of the twentieth century and which has recently returned to the presidency after an absence of twelve years.

In some respects the conflicts of twentieth-century Mexico had their origin in the colonial period when Mexico was part of the Spanish monarchy. The Catholic Church became an instrument of government under the Spaniards, and it also supplied much of the leadership of Mexican society, including the priest leaders who shook off Spanish rule.

After independence, the church was allied with conservative forces in Mexican society. When the French-backed Hapsburg Emperor of Mexico, Maximilian, was overthrown by Benito Juarez (with US support) in 1867, most of the church's privileges and property were taken away.

It is therefore something of a mystery as to why the 'Liberal' generals – who forty years later led the Revolution of 1910 – were still so hostile to the Catholic Church, seeking to licence and limit the activities of priests and close church schools.

This led to a bloody guerrilla war, chiefly in western Mexico, where lightly armed but mobile 'Cristeros' defied the battle-hardened but immobile Mexican army for years. Some of these same passions regarding the boundaries and overlap between religion and politics arose in the Spanish Civil War, which broke out in 1936, only a few years after the Cristero rebellion had finally ended. Many of the republican losers in the Spanish Civil War found refuge in Mexico, and their descendants remain influential in Mexican life.

Like all Latin American countries, a major theme in Mexican history is the relationship between the European settlers and the Native American populations. In some countries, like Argentina and Uruguay, the natives were almost wiped out by disease and land grabbing. In Mexico, the native population was reduced to almost a fifth of its former size by the introduction of European diseases, to which the natives had no immunity. As a result of this loss, Mexico and Ireland had the same population in 1840 – eight million people.

Land rights were a hugely contentious issue. The natives asserted ancient rights to common land, while the modernising European or mixed-race farmers wanted to take that land for commercial production. Interestingly, the Emperor Maximilian gave more support to native land rights than any of Mexico's own leaders, including the man who overthrew and executed Maximilian, Benito Juarez, who was himself of native blood.

Mexico is one of the emerging economic powers of the world, and understanding its history is important.

ROBERT PEEL:
A POLITICIAN UNAFRAID TO CHANGE HIS MIND

Robert Peel: A Biography,
Douglas Hurd (Phoenix 2008)

Robert Peel was elected to the UK Parliament at the age of twenty-one, for a constituency in which only twenty-four people had a vote. That constituency was Cashel, in County Tipperary, and the year was 1809.

He went on to become Prime Minister of the United Kingdom, to form the first professional police force in the world, to reintroduce income tax at seven pence in the pound, and to split his own party and end his own career by enacting a law to reduce the duty on corn imports.

These are the highlights of the career of Sir Robert Peel, the subject of an excellent biography by Douglas Hurd.

As a former Conservative politician himself (he was Secretary of State for Northern Ireland, as well as Foreign Secretary and Home Secretary during the 1980s), Douglas Hurd has a natural sympathy with Peel. He is also able to draw apt comparisons between events in Peel's career and events in modern politics.

Peel at first opposed Catholic Emancipation (which allowed Catholics to sit in the House of Commons), but he eventually came around to supporting it. He also initially opposed parliamentary reform. This reform was justified because, when Peel first came into Parliament in 1809, big cities like Birmingham and Manchester had no MPs at all, while Old Sarum, a place with no electors, had an MP to represent it.

When he established the Metropolitan Police, he decided that there would be no 'officer corps' with separate entry requirements, like there was in the army and the navy. In this respect, his decision endures to this day in both Ireland and Britain, where promotion to top ranks in the police is open to all entry-level recruits, in ways that it is not in the military in either country.

The repeal of the Corn Laws in 1846 was the most significant event of Peel's career. His party represented farming interests, and most of his supporters wanted to keep a high duty on foreign corn, so as to keep the price high for their own produce. Peel felt that this led to unacceptably high food prices in towns, and particularly in Ireland, where the potato blight was beginning to take its toll.

The only way Peel could get his Corn Law repeal bill through Parliament was with the help of opposition MPs and the votes of a minority of his own party MPs. The majority of his own party turned against him. While the bill to repeal the protectionist Corn Laws was passed, its passage ended Robert Peel's political career.

Douglas Hurd portrays Peel as an unemotional and aloof politician, who made his decisions on the basis of careful and open-minded study of facts and figures, rather than on political instinct.

AS TENSION MOUNTS IN UKRAINE: SALUTARY LESSONS FROM 1914

The Sleepwalkers: How Europe Went to War in 1914,
Christopher Clark (Harper, 2013)

The Sleepwalkers: How Europe Went to War in 1914 by Christopher Clark, Professor of Modern History at Cambridge, describes the statesmen who stumbled into war in 1914 as 'sleepwalkers, watchful but unseeing, haunted by dreams, yet blind to the horror they were about to bring to the world'.

A web of interlocking commitments, designed to give individual countries security and peace behind their own borders, ended up dragging the whole continent into war.

Austria–Hungary had a defensive pact with Germany. Russia set itself up as the protector of Serbia. France gave Russia a blank cheque in the Balkans because it needed Russian assurances against Germany. Britain had a rather more vague understanding with France. It feared any Russian rapprochement with Germany because Russia could threaten British interests in India.

So, when Archduke Franz Ferdinand was murdered in Sarajevo by Serbian assassins, the possibility that all these dominoes might fall in the direction of war opened up. But it was only a possibility.

Serbia could have taken resolute action to root out the conspiracy behind the assassins before Austria issued any ultimatum. Austria could have issued a more temperate ultimatum.

Serbia could have given a less evasive response. Germany could have restrained Austria. Russia could have held back from full-scale mobilisation in support of Serbia, and France could have made it clear that it did not wish to get involved in supporting a Russian attack on Austria, so long as Germany stayed out too. Britain could have said it would remain neutral in a German war with France, so long as Germany respected Belgian neutrality.

But none of these things happened.

The interlocking commitments between countries that led to war were not, according to Christopher Clark, 'long-term features of the European system, but the consequence of numerous short-term adjustments' made in the immediately preceding years.

The war was not inevitable, but it suited some leaders to pretend afterwards that it was, so as to avoid facing the consequences of some of their own omissions, ambiguities and evasions.

Some of the issues involved are still relevant today.

For example, how does one pursue a criminal conspiracy launched from another jurisdiction? If the European Arrest Warrant was in place in 1914, could Austria have secured the extradition of some of the conspirators from Belgrade without threatening war?

Christopher Clark says Austria's ultimatum to Serbia was milder than the one NATO issued to Serbia in 1999. Luckily, the NATO ultimatum did not have the same dire consequences.

As we see an escalating confrontation between Russia and the West, the lesson I draw from this book is that leaders must not think solely of the next move, but of the likely counter move, the move after that and so on, bearing in mind that nothing is inevitable until it has actually happened, and that they usually have more choices than they are willing to acknowledge.

THE BARD OF ERIN:
A MAN OF MANY PARTS

∽

Bard of Erin: The Life of Thomas Moore,
Ronan Kelly (Penguin, 2008)

I remember, as a child, playing over and over again the records of John McCormack's songs. The records had belonged to my deceased grand-uncle, John. Many of the songs in the great Irish tenor's repertoire had been written over one hundred years prior to McCormack's time, by another Irishman, the poet and author, Thomas Moore. They were widely known as 'Moore's Melodies'.

I knew little else about Moore, although I remember I had a stamp, in my now long-lost stamp collection, which had been issued in his honour in 1952. So it was with only mild interest that I picked up a copy of Ronan Kelly's biography of Moore in a Dublin bookshop. I am glad I did.

Moore was born in Aungier Street in Dublin in 1779, to a Catholic merchant family. His mother's people, the Codds, were from Wexford, and the Moores were from Kerry.

He was privately educated, and went to Trinity College, Dublin at the age of fifteen. In order to pursue his literary career, he went to England after finishing college, and never returned permanently to Ireland.

The Moore that emerges from these pages is much more than a mere sentimental and patriotic balladeer. In fact, the melodies themselves were not Moore's work at all, but had been collected by Edward Bunting from traditional local sources. Moore composed words to accompany the melodies, thus giving life and meaning to them. From these compositions came his celebrity, and much of his badly needed income.

As well as being the author of popular songs, Moore was a substantial poet, and friend of other poets, like Byron, Shelley, Rogers and Wordsworth. He was an active political satirist, supporting the Whig party against the Tories.

He was also a biographer and historian, writing biographies of Lord Byron and Richard Brinsley Sheridan. He was so close to Byron that Byron entrusted him with his own autobiography – a work that was destroyed, unpublished, after Byron's untimely death, because of a dispute between Moore and some of Byron's friends.

Moore wrote a substantial history of Ireland, and his poetry was accompanied by comprehensive explanatory footnotes – the fruit of extensive historical research.

In England, Moore's literary fame enabled him to become friends with many members of the Whig aristocracy, including Lord Lansdowne and the future Prime Minister, Lord John Russell. He was the recipient of political patronage from the Whigs, notably a sinecure in Bermuda adjudicating on the ownership of captured cargoes.

Although he cultivated an English accent and married a Protestant, he remained an active critic of British rule in Ireland and a supporter of Catholic Emancipation. He considered himself 'English' when visiting America or France, but 'Irish' when he was living in England.

Because Moore wrote so much, both for publication and in private letters and diaries, Ronan Kelly's research presents a deep insight into the attitudes and lifestyle of a generation of Irish people who had experienced the 1798 rebellion, the Act of Union, and the struggle for Catholic Emancipation, but had yet to absorb the full horror and bitter political fruits of the Famine. It opens a window into another world.

THE NATURE OF MONEY, AND HOW CREATING MORE OF IT CAN BE BOTH GOOD AND BAD

The Ascent of Money: A Financial History of the World,
Niall Ferguson (Penguin, 2009)

In his book, *The Ascent of Money*, the historian Niall Ferguson tells the story of the development of money – a means of exchange that depends on trust – from its earliest origins in ancient Mesopotamia, when clay tokens were used, through the dominance of gold in the later Middle Ages, where the supply of gold limited the amount of money that could be in circulation, and to the key landmark in monetary evolution: the scrapping of usury laws in 1833, which allowed for an expansion of interest-bearing loans and paper money. Money became credit. Today, thanks to this development, 95% of the money we use is bank credit and only 5% or less is cash.

Gradually the amount of purchasing power in the economy came to bear less and less on the relationship to the reserves of gold or other capital that was supposed to back it all up.

There were many frauds, scares and panics along the way. The historical episodes described in Ferguson's book discredit the mathematical models of finance, which purport to predict human behaviour on the basis of past performance.

They enhance the credibility of the 'reflexivity' theory of hedge fund owner George Soros, who sees market behaviour as a 'reflection' of the irrational hopes, fears, and biases of millions of half-informed people.

Recent financial history, with its succession of bubbles and busts, shows that the auditors, non-executive directors, and regulators, who are supposed to be diligent, get carried away by irrational hopes and fears, just like everyone else.

Niall Ferguson, who is himself a professor at Harvard, says that in 1970 only 5% of the men graduating from Harvard went into banking and finance. By 2007, 20% of the men and 10% of the women were doing so. One started to get too much of a good thing. The ever-more creative forms of credit offered by the expanded financial sector fuelled a consumption boom in the US. Consumer spending jumped from 62% of income in the 1960s to 74% in 2006. Household savings almost completely disappeared.

This development was made easy by the sudden easing of the movement of money across the world. The huge savings that Chinese factory workers had to accumulate, because they had no welfare state to fall back on if they lost their jobs, were recycled into consumer loans, which enabled Americans to buy more Chinese goods than they could afford.

The Ascent of Money puts our present anxieties in a historical context and would provide useful background reading for the Irish Banking Enquiry.

THE ORIGINS AND FUTURE ON NATIONALISM

Irish Freedom: The History of Nationalism in Ireland,
Richard English (Pan MacMillan, 2008)

The excellent book, *Irish Freedom: The History of Nationalism in Ireland* by Richard English, a Belfast academic, places Irish nationalism in the context of the development of nationalist ideas elsewhere.

Most writers date the emergence of nationalism as an ideology to the French Revolution, which proclaimed that 'each people is independent and sovereign'. This thinking originated with the English philosopher John Locke, who said that political power should rest on the consent of the governed, rather than on the divine right of kings.

But if consent is to be given, people have to be organised into units that can give or withhold consent. Thus came about the creation of 'nations'. The difficulty was, and remains, in defining the boundaries of these nations. This was especially so when populations and allegiances were mixed, as in Ireland.

The problem in the Irish case was recognised as early as 1907, by a nationalist writer, Arthur Clery, who wrote, 'You can no more talk Protestant Ulster into Irishry, than Ireland can be argued into Englishry.' The 1916 leaders, in proclaiming a republic, made no effort whatsoever to deal with this problem.

Indeed that reality was ignored by most Irish nationalists, in both parts of the island, until recently. Even to this day, the Good Friday Agreement is held by many to be a transitional step on the road to an eventual United Ireland, on the presumption that, despite all the evidence to the contrary, Ulster Protestants will eventually be 'talked into Irishry'.

The Sinn Féin thinker Tom Hartley told the author in 2001 that, when the Troubles began, Sinn Féin thought of Unionists as a 'non people': 'We didn't even see them as part of the problem, never mind part of the solution,' he admitted.

This thoughtful self-criticism by an Irish Republican is a big change from the attitude of Roger Casement who, hoping in 1912 for German victory in the expected war, said, 'I pray for the Germans and their coming. A Protestant power to teach these Protestants their place in Irish life, is what is needed.'

Catholicism was not always as important a part of the Irish nationalist self-identity as it was later to become. Many United Irishmen were Protestant, but seemingly no Protestant was among the 917 rebels detained in the 1917–19 period.

Violence divided people radically, and forced them into camps. In 1968, 20% of Ulster Protestants described themselves as 'Irish', but by 1986, after fifteen years of IRA violence, only 3% did so.

Land was important too. By taking back the land and ending landlordism in 1903, the conquest of Northern Ireland was partially 'repealed', even before a shot was fired.

This long book, while timely and interesting, does not really explore the alternatives to nationalism as an organising principle for human governance. Richard English argues that nationalism has outlasted other ideologies, like Communism, because it answered the basic human need for belonging, self-respect and security. Nationalism worked with the grain of human nature, rather than against it.

On the other hand, nationalism is new in historic terms. The use of religion rather than ethnicity as a way of uniting people has been around much longer. Islam is a modern example with many historic antecedents. It is arguable that 'western values' and 'the rule of law' may take over from nationalism as the binding force in Europe. After all, before nationalism was discovered, successful multi-ethnic empires – like the Austro-Hungarian, Ottoman and Byzantine empires – provided stability for hundreds of years.

Modern thinking is that people can hold within themselves several national identities at once, just as more and more people now have two passports, for example an Irish and an American passport. This sort of multiple identity will increase in the future, because there are increasing numbers of marriages between people of different nationalities.

Furthermore, the now well-established idea of universal human rights does not sit easily with the nationalist doctrine of 'my country right or wrong'.

World Politics

A TWO-STATE SOLUTION?

The preferred solution the international community has for the dispute between Israelis and Palestinians is two states, one Israeli and one Palestinian, existing side by side, with international guarantees. One of these states, the Palestinian one, would be demilitarised while the other, Israel, would presumably remain a fully armed nuclear power.

As of now, the Palestinian and Israeli populations are roughly equal in number. Israel proper has 78% of the territory. This leaves 22% for the Palestinians. Israelis continue to build settlements in the 22% left to the Palestinians.

In fact, the rate of population increase among the Israeli settlers who have moved into this small 22% share of the original territory of Palestine (the occupied territories) is much faster than is the rate of population growth among Israelis who live in the 78% share of original Palestine that is Israel proper.

One does not have to be a brilliant mathematician to work out that if this trend continues, a two-state solution will become physically and geographically impossible.

There would be no manageable space left in which to found a Palestinian state. Little islands of Palestinian land, cut off from one another by Israeli roads, settlements and security barriers, would not leave the Palestinians with a territory over which they could realistically be expected to establish a sovereign state capable of taking on the responsibilities of control over its own territory, and the respect for its neighbours, that sovereignty implies.

President Obama asked the Israeli government to stop settlement building in the Palestinian territories. Israel has declined to do so. There have been no consequences for Israel as a result of this refusal.

The United States continues to buy arms from Israel. Israel remains the largest per capita recipient of US foreign aid, although it is a prosperous country. Americans can claim tax relief on financial contributions they make to Israeli settlement activity, even though their President has asked for it to stop.

I believe a perception of inequitable treatment of Palestinians has an effect on attitudes towards the West in countries with large Muslim populations.

I also believe that it has contributed, indirectly, to the decline in the Christian populations in Middle Eastern countries. It assists in creating a sense of injustice among Muslims that helps the recruitment of terrorist organisations.

The Civil Rights Movement in the United States initially focused on the equal right to vote. So too did that in Northern Ireland.

Palestinians living in the West Bank have no right to vote on the composition of the government that, in reality, controls their lives – the Israeli government. While that situation can be sustained militarily, it cannot be sustained politically. The indefinite continuance of this situation puts supporters of Israel, who believe in democracy for all, in a false position. That is not wise from an Israeli point of view.

Serious pursuit of a two-state solution would resolve that contradiction, so long as what is to be created is a genuinely sovereign Palestinian state. I doubt if the pursuit of a two-state solution would be seen as serious as long as Israeli settlement activity in the 22% potential territory of a Palestinian state continues. I do not know how long this anomaly can persist, perhaps for a long time, but the ultimate result will be tragic for all.

Arguably, a one-state solution, in which all Palestinians vote in Israeli elections, is being rendered more likely by the failure of the Israeli government to accept the logic of a two-state solution.

I first posted these reflections on the Palestinian/Israeli issue on my website in January 2010. Unfortunately what I wrote then remains completely relevant today. The official goal of a two-state solution is no nearer now than it was then.

CHINA, EUROPE AND THE POLITICAL ECONOMY OF THE WORLD

In September 2013 I visited China to speak at a meeting of Zhejiang Chamber of Commerce at the Guangzhou Baiyun International Convention Centre. The last time I had been in Guangzhou was in 1978 when, as a relatively young member of the Irish legislature, I went to observe the beginning of the modernisation of China, under the leadership of the late Chairman Deng.

My impression, at the time, was that everybody travelled by bicycle and wore uniform clothes. The sound of China for me was the tinkle of a thousand bicycle bells. China struck me as a sensibly frugal society, which left nothing go to waste. There was a sense of order, a sense that people knew where they were going.

I also found people who were immensely welcoming towards a European like myself, who came from a continent whose interactions with China over the previous 150 years had often been marked, on the European side, by exploitation and racism.

I even saw the remnants of the European concessions in Guangzhou, where, until 1949, European nations applied their own rules, even though this was Chinese sovereign territory. In what had once been the French concession, I came across a disused Catholic church that had been converted into a clothing factory. I sometimes wonder if it has since been restored to its former use.

I also had a strong sense, then, that China was a society on the move.

Thirty-five years later, I was back in a very different city, in one of the great commercial centres of the world, to see the results of the modernisation initiated by the Four Modernisations policy of 1978.

The Four Modernisations
Many people at the time may have thought that the Four Modernisations, the policy of Deng, were only rhetoric.

I came across a phrase recently which sums up the Four Modernisations policy: the country was 'wading across a river, by feeling for stones underfoot'.

In other words, it was a policy of experimentation, of trial and error; allowing mistakes to be made, trying different approaches in different regions, and allowing competition between the different approaches and the different regions.

This flexibility explains the difference between Chinese and Soviet economic policy at that time, and explains why the first succeeded where the other failed.

Indeed, the strength of the western capitalist economic model is that it also encourages experimentation and trial and error, but uses different methods to do so.

China has made huge strides since 1978. It is now well established as a middle-income country, according to World Bank classifications.

From a middle-income country to a high-income country
In 1960, there were one hundred middle-income countries in the world. Ireland was one of them.

By 2008, only thirteen of those one hundred countries had reached high-income status. Ireland was one of the thirteen that made it, alongside Hong Kong, Japan, South Korea, Mauritius, Spain, Equatorial Guinea, Portugal and Greece. Note the inclusion of Greece in this list!

The remaining eighty-seven middle-income countries in 1960 have undoubtedly made progress since, but they are still middle-income countries. In fact, some of those who attained high-income status by 2008 may now be falling back into the middle-income category.

Nothing stands still. Progress is not automatic. Economic growth is, as the economist Schumpeter put it, 'a process of constant creative destruction'. Growth is about change. Change is often painful, and painful but necessary change can easily be confused with mindless austerity.

When a country is moving from less-developed to middle-income status, it is often able to compete by doing things more cheaply than established competitors can do them. There is no need to come up with brand new technologies. It can use existing technologies, but apply them at less cost and with minor improvements.

Moving a country from middle-income to high-income status, in contrast, often requires it to push at the very boundaries of technology, to find a niche that no one else is filling, to invest in people and ideas, as well as in concrete and metal.

That is the demanding stage into which China is now moving its 1.4 billion people, a move that promises to be one of the great transformations of human history.

Engines of economic growth

The size of the transformation involved explains why China is today spending 2% of its GDP on Research and Development (R&D), which is more, as a proportion of GDP, than Ireland, the Netherlands, the UK, Norway, Luxembourg, Italy, Spain, and many other European countries are spending.

Incidentally, Israel, South Korea, and Finland are the biggest proportionate spenders in the world on R&D. But R&D alone will not move a country from middle- to high-income status. Entrepreneurs must be able to use the results of that R&D by setting up new businesses and recruiting talented local people to help them do it.

Here, Ireland has a strong advantage in that it is one of the easiest places in Europe to set up a new business, and one of the easiest in which to recruit young, well-educated people at competitive salaries.

This has already attracted eighteen different Chinese companies to set up operation in Ireland. Ireland is particularly interested in Chinese companies operating in fields like life sciences, clean tech, financial services and information technology.

Ireland is also active in food exports to China, which have grown by 92% in just two years.

I believe there are aspects of the Irish educational system from which China could benefit. 5,000 Chinese students study in Ireland. Numerous agreements exist between Irish and Chinese universities. These must be built upon, especially in key areas of research, like financial services.

Removing blockages in the system
If China is to exploit its investment in R&D to the full, it needs to liberalise its system of local residency permits, which discourage migration within China, and to make it easier for new Chinese companies to start up and compete with existing state-owned or established enterprises.

The European Union, with its 0.5 billion people, is a much smaller entity than China with its 1.4 billion people. But in the European Union, there are still restrictions on internal migration, analogous to the Chinese residency permit scheme, in that the EU does not have full transferability of social security rights or full mutual recognition of professional qualifications for internal migrants within the EU.

The danger of property bubbles: the Irish experience
But it would be unrealistic for me not to refer to some of the recent economic difficulties Ireland has encountered.

These difficulties are being overcome. Growth has been resumed, foreign investment in the country is at an all-time high, and the government is following a careful plan. But it is also important to objectively analyse how Ireland got into these difficulties, and I believe that would be helpful to a country, like China, that is also undergoing rapid development, and wants to avoid converting that into a destructive bubble.

Indeed, the latest IMF report on China contains warnings that will sound familiar to those who have studied recent Irish economic history.

It talks of the risks of 'a steady build-up of leverage eroding the strength of the financial sector', of 'a boom in non-traditional sources of credit', and of the need to take 'steps to reduce moral hazard to ensure that banks do not engage in potentially destabilising competition'. On the other hand, it recognises that China has very well capitalised banks.

A few years ago, these very risks existed in Ireland, and were not adequately addressed by the authorities in Ireland, or in the European Union. We have suffered for that, and these are useful lessons for China now.

This is what happened in Ireland. Thanks to artificially cheap credit and rapidly rising property prices, Ireland experienced a property bubble between 2000 and 2007. This bubble led to a radical distortion of the country's economic structures, and to a big increase in private and government debt.

The cheap credit was available because of decisions taken by the US Federal Reserve and the European Central Bank. Both favoured low interest rates. They did so to avoid dislocations to the economy that might have arisen from the dot-com burst, 9/11, and the costs of German reunification.

In these goals they succeeded.

But the extra credit also found its way across national boundaries into housing markets in various countries, causing a bubble in prices, most notably in Ireland. In 2008, the bubble burst.

Bubbles distort the economy
The bubble distorted the Irish economy in ways that will take years to repair. There was distortion in the form of

- A doubling in the size of the construction sector,
- Large and uncompetitive pay increases across the economy, and,
- Rapid increases in the number of people employed in the public sector.

The fact that money was flowing in, temporarily, to government coffers made it hard to resist demands to increase the size of the government sector permanently.

In just five years, from 2001 to 2006, the share of the workforce in the public sector in Ireland reached 29%, as against 19% in Germany. The numbers in top-grade positions in the civil service grew by 86%.

Instead of choosing careers and skills for which there is enduring global demand, talented people were drawn into activities for which demand is inherently temporary, like construction.

Why bubbles happen
In a way, it is easy to see why people made the mistake of thinking that house prices in Ireland (and household wealth) would never stop rising. Recent history seemed to suggest that the only way house prices could go was up.

House prices had already risen by 133% between 1994 and 2000. These increases were actually justified by rapid economic growth, immigration, and new family formation, all of which created a genuine demand for housing. People got used to house prices rising faster than other prices, and came to assume that this was a natural condition that would continue indefinitely.

The trouble is that the overly rapid increase in house prices continued after 2000, when it was no longer justified by additional demand. Worse still, it was financed, not by improved competitiveness, but by excessive lending, and by income generated from inherently temporary construction spending.

It is clear that the bankers who were lending this money seemed to think that demand for housing could keep growing forever. A moment's thought would have shown how nonsensical that was.

But, in the middle of a boom, people are often too busy to stop and think.

The revenue of the government became unhealthily dependent on taxes derived from property sales such as stamp duty, capital gains tax, and VAT on house sales. Property-related revenues reached 18% of all revenues in 2006, whereas they had only been 8% in 2002.

But once house sales slowed down, of course, that revenue growth stopped, leaving a huge hole in the government's budget.

Again, a moment's thought would have shown how dangerous it was to build up permanent spending programmes on the back of inherently temporary streams of revenue. But very few people, in politics or outside it, took a moment to think.

Countries like China must look to Ireland and ask, 'How can sensible, and generally public-spirited, people make mistakes like this, and how can such mistakes be avoided?'

The causes of bubbles: silo thinking and following fashion without reflection
I would identify two tendencies of policy making in both the public and private sector that were at the heart of the problem in Ireland.

1. 'Silo mentalities' within institutions, which is when groups don't share in formation with each other and instead focus only on their own immediate responsibilities.
2. A 'consensus approach', which encouraged a single view to be taken of any issue. Human beings are followers of fashion.

We need institutions that deliberately challenge fashionable assumptions, and unfortunately institutions in Ireland and in the wider European Union did not deliver.

These errors can occur in *any* country, under *any* political system. They are not unique to Ireland, Spain, the US, or any of the other parts of the world where property bubbles arose.

China must be vigilant if they want to keep these problems from their economy, and I know the authorities are fully aware of these risks.

The global challenges: ageing, migration, climate change, an eroding tax base, and sound finance
These are the five big problems that the countries of the world must come together to tackle., and they are all loosely related to one another. With the exception of the finance issue, they are all problems that are silently creeping up on us, so silently in fact that it is difficult to create a sufficient sense of immediate crisis to get anything done about them.

Technology will provide some of the answers, and China is devoting a significant proportion of its R&D to some of these issues. But sacrifices, and compromises, will be needed between (and within) nations if these problems are to be met. Pension entitlements will have to be limited, working lives extended, and elder care vastly expanded with the aid of technology. Migration will have to be accepted in ageing economies, and that is a big cultural challenge. CO_2 emissions and pollution will have to be tackled by making the polluter meet the full cost of what he does.

We may eventually need some form of global taxation to meet the cost of preserving our common global heritage, but in the meantime we need to restore the tax base of states in a co-operative way. We cannot expect government to function if its revenues are artificially depleted.

And finally we need to put banking on a footing that will allow incompetent banks to be closed down, without putting the whole economy at risk. 'Too big to fail' and 'too interconnected to fail' should no longer be characteristics of our banking systems.

The euro: what is its future?
The existence of the euro, the single currency, has not created the economic crisis in Europe. This was going to come anyway because of lost competitiveness, the emergence of new competitors – like China – for traditional European industries, and the progressive ageing of European societies.

Expansionary monetary policy postponed the emergence of the symptoms; it could *not* have prevented the illness.

What the existence of the euro has done is impose discipline and mutual solidarity on Europe. Without the euro, countries would have pursued the route of devaluation and inflation in response to their present problems. Savings would have been wiped out. That is not possible now, which is a good thing. Instead, problems are now being tackled at their source.

Without the euro, wealthier and stronger European countries would not have come so quickly to the aid of other European countries in difficulty. They have now done so on a systematic basis, and that too is good.

The EU is moving towards a common system for winding up banks that need to be wound up, without putting the overall system at risk. It is moving, I hope, towards a common system of deposit insurance. These are issues that also require attention in China.

Much better systems are now being put in place in the European Union to ensure that in future, public finances, and underlying competitiveness, do not get out of line again.

As a result of the crisis, we are now facing up to problems we had ignored for the past twenty years in Europe.

The euro will survive. Not only that, I believe it will eventually be imitated in other parts of the world.

To sum up, the euro is

- A protection against the expropriation of savings, through inflation and devaluation,
- A factor for economic stability in the world, and,
- A major political step forward for unity in Europe.

Based on a speech I made at a meeting of Zhejiang Chamber of Commerce at the Guangzhou Baiyun International Convention Centre in September 2013.

THE WAY HOUSE OF REPRESENTATIVES DISTRICT BOUNDARIES ARE SET IS A CORE CAUSE OF DEADLOCK IN US POLITICS

Many in Europe assume that the only really important election in the United States is the presidential election. But a President who cannot get his/her legislative programme enacted by both Houses of Congress can achieve little, at least in domestic politics – something President Obama is now learning.

In fact, the relative positioning of the candidates in the presidential race is influenced by problems in Congress. Hillary Clinton is way ahead of other potential rivals for the Democratic nomination, if she decides to run. Indeed the polls are so decisive that she would find it very hard not to do so. But there is a strong possibility that, if elected, she will face a Congress where at least one of the Houses is controlled by the Republicans.

On the Republican side, Rand Paul and Mike Huckabee show up best in polls in a widely dispersed field. But close observers suggest that Jeb Bush has the best chance of coming through as eventual Republican nominee, because he has a position on immigration that would allow him to win back Hispanic votes. These are votes that his brother George W. got when he was elected. This is important, because the Hispanic support that George W. Bush won has since been lost to the party because Republicans, who have a majority in the House of Representatives, refuse to vote on an Immigration Reform Bill that has already passed in the Senate.

The Republican Speaker of the House, John Boehner, will not schedule a vote because, although the Bill has an overall majority in the House, it lacks a majority within the Republican majority itself.

This 'majority of the majority' requirement, which has been the approach of Republicans since they won a House majority, makes it very difficult to pass any bipartisan legislation.

Many Republicans in the House were elected on a platform of 'no compromise', and are fearful of being undermined by Tea Party candidates in their party primaries.

This means that they are also refusing to vote for any tax changes to reduce the deficit. The only tax changes they will support are pure tax cuts.

Likewise Congress has, until now, prevented President Obama from getting the authority to negotiate a trade deal to be voted on in Congress as a single package (so-called 'Fast Track' authority, without which any meaningful trade negotiation is almost impossible).

The problem here is in President Obama's own Democratic Party. The pattern of polarisation in US politics has meant that, while Republican House members in safe Republican districts are disproportionately influenced by the Tea Party wing, Democrat House members in safe Democratic districts are often disproportionately under the influence of the unions, and some unions are strongly against freer trade. Now that the Republicans control both Houses of Congress, it looks as if President Obama may get, from his political enemies, the trade negotiation authority that he was so long denied by his political allies.

Congress is also blocking an agreement on a reweighting of quotas between IMF countries to reflect new global realities. They are refusing to recognise the new weight countries like China have in the world. In fact, a complete reform package for IMF voting powers – to give proper recognition to the increased economic weight of emerging economies, while protecting the voting rights of the poorest countries, and to make the Executive board of the IMF more representative, which has the support of 77% of existing members – cannot come into effect because of a longstanding veto in the US Congress.

This deadlock is a frustration for everybody, including the international partners of the United States. The underlying problem is in the way districts are drawn for House of Representatives elections. The districts are not decided at national level, but are drawn up by the state legislatures. In most states, the legislatures design congressional districts to create totally safe seats for one party or the other, and ensure that sitting members are not thrown together in the same one-seat district.

This means that districts often have highly contorted boundaries, and it also means that the really important contest for House elections is in primaries within parties, rather than in general elections.

So House members spend their time fundraising to fend off opponents from within their own party. They are particularly fearful of a rival who might advocate a more fundamentalist view point. There is no electoral incentive to seek middle-ground support. That then affects the way members of Congress approach votes in House itself.

There are two ways to resolve this dilemma.

One would be to hand over the drawing of the Congressional district boundaries to an independent commission in each state, which would draw the lines on the basis of geographical convenience without trying to create safe seats for particular parties. This is already done in seven states.

The other is to have 'Open Primaries', where voters, of all parties and none, would take part in selecting the top two candidates who would contest one another in the general election. The top two candidates would then run against one another in the general election, even if both happened to come from the same party.

Both of these solutions would mean that candidates for the House would have an incentive to look for middle-ground support, rather than just court their own hardcore 'base'.

Such solutions could only be brought about on a state by state basis. They could not be imposed on a blanket basis in all states because that would interfere with 'states' rights', a strong tradition in US politics for over two hundred years.

It is often said that the European Union needs a Constitutional Convention to revise its constituting treaties. The same could be said of the United States of America.

I first posted these reflections on US politics on my website in May 2014. Things have not improved since, except on trade policy.

THE EU SHOULD TAKE THE US TO INTERNATIONAL COURT IF SNOWDEN ALLEGATIONS ARE VALID

∽

Allegations that the United States National Security Agency was bugging the premises of the EU delegation in Washington and other EU offices first appeared in July 2013. The following was my reaction to this at the time. Nothing has happened to change my view of the illegality of what was revealed then.

Edward Snowden's allegations that the United States National Security Agency (NSA), for which he worked, spied on diplomatic missions of the European Union in Washington and New York, and even on the building where EU Summits take place in Brussels, are very serious. The fact that Snowden may have had deeply unpatriotic motives for releasing this information does not reduce their seriousness.

These undenied allegations require a deliberate and sustained response from the European Union, not something exaggerated, or that will last only for a one-day news cycle, and later expose contradictions in the EU positions.

The truth is that fundamental values are at stake here for the EU.

The founding idea of the EU was that relations in and between member states should be governed by rules, rather than by raw power, as had previously been the case. States, and individuals, should be equal before the law.

The Snowden allegations, if true, reveal a grave breach in international law by an agency of the United States government.

This is not something that can be deplored in the short term, and be then later brushed aside with a worldly wise and jaded shrug, saying 'everyone is at it'.

A clear breach of three articles of the Vienna Convention
The Vienna Convention of 1961 codifies the rules under which diplomats and embassies do their work. But the rules themselves go back, in customary international law, to the sixteenth century.

The 1961 Vienna Convention has been ratified by the United States. Indeed, the US relied on that Convention in the International Court of Justice, when its own diplomats and Embassy were interfered with by Iran in 1979.

It is in the national interest of the United States to ensure that this Convention is respected, without question, and as a matter of routine, in order to ensure protection for its own missions abroad.

The Vienna Convention says, in Article 22, 'the premises of a [diplomatic] mission shall be inviolable', and, 'a receiving state shall not enter them, except with the consent of the Head of Mission'. 'The receiving state is under a special duty to take all appropriate steps to protect the premises of the mission from any intrusion.'

Article 24 of the Convention says the 'archives and documents of the mission shall be inviolable' and Article 27 extends similar protection to its correspondence.

The Snowden/*Der Spiegel* allegations suggest that listening devices were placed in the EU mission in Washington, without consent, which would be a blatant breach of Article 22.

They also suggest that the NSA hacked into the computer system of the EU missions, which would be a clear breach of both Articles 24 and 27 of the Vienna Convention.

Reacting to these allegations, US figures, including the former head of the CIA, made no reference at all to US obligations under international law, to US interest in protecting diplomacy, or even to the unfairness and bad faith involved in spying on negotiation partners. Instead they sought to dismiss them, by hinting vaguely about intelligence gathering by some EU states.

But this is not a case of the US reciprocally countering supposed illegal activities by some EU states. It was hostile and illegal activity by the US, directed against the EU itself. The EU does not have either the capacity or the authority to carry out any reciprocal surveillance of US missions in Europe, and does not do so.

In any event, I do not understand the point of what the NSA was supposedly doing.

The activities of the EU missions abroad, and of the Council of Ministers in Brussels, deal with subjects on which the facts are well known, and on which negotiating options are also fairly obvious.

They can be easily discovered by US officials, simply by asking. They do not involve sensitive questions concerning the security of the United States, which is supposed to be the concern of the NSA.

There will, very occasionally, be commercially sensitive and confidential information shared with the EU mission in Washington by European or American companies, which might be useful to its competitors. Apart from the illegality involved, the NSA would have no legitimate reason to seek out, collect, or share that sort of commercial information.

I believe what is involved here is a case of a security bureaucracy gradually extending its role, and engaging in 'mission creep' just because it can and because nobody is stopping it. The missions of agencies are often lazily defined and open to multiple interpretations. That may well be the case with the NSA.

Trade and investment talks should continue
What should the EU do now? I will start by saying what it should not do. It should not suspend the negotiation of a possible Trade and Investment Pact with the United States. In fact, it should recognise that these allegations strengthen the EU's hand in these negotiations, in the sense that the US now has to demonstrate its good faith.

Nor should it expect an early, full, or contrite admission from the United States of what might have happened, or make that a precondition for anything.

Instead, the EU should adopt a twin-track approach. It should continue with the trade and investment negotiations as if nothing had happened. But, simultaneously and separately, the EU and its member states should follow the example set by the United States itself in 1980, and take a case in regard to these allegations to the International Court of Justice in the Hague.

This assumes that it can obtain sufficient documentary evidence of the Snowden allegations from Mr Snowden, or from *Der Spiegel*.

Pursuing a legal route would depoliticise the issue in the short term, and allow time for things to cool down.

Surveillance technology has advanced a great deal since 1961, when the Convention was concluded. A new judgement from the International Court in this case would be helpful. It would re-establish and modernise the norms of behaviour we would want all countries to respect in future, notably emerging powers like China.

President Obama, who, probably more than any previous President, understands the significance of international law should welcome such a robust reaffirmation of the Vienna Convention.

Religion

A REFLECTION AT EASTER TIME

Faith was one of the great gifts afforded to my generation, born in Ireland in the years after the Second World War. It is a gift we have an obligation to pass on.

Our faith tells us that there is a God; that we are not alone in the universe. We should not be arrogant. We should respect His creation. We should leave the earth in a better condition than we found it. There is something out there greater than us, so we can and must keep our own troubles in proportion.

Our faith tells us that God created each one of us as individuals, that we are not mere accidents of genetics, and that He cares for each of us, as individuals. Our life comes from Him, and it is not ours to manipulate, or take away.

Our faith tells us that there is a life after our death; we do not simply pass away into nothingness. We have to give an account of ourselves.

But our faith also tells us that God sent His only Son to die on earth, so that our sins would be forgiven, and that we might live.

These beliefs are, I contend, as important to the living of a good life now, in twenty-first century Ireland, as they ever were at any time in our country's long history since Christianity was first introduced to this island in the fifth century.

As Pope Benedict said in his encyclical *Caritas in Veritate*, 'Deeds without knowledge are blind, and knowledge without love is sterile.'

Science and material progress are only means to an end, no more. They are not why we are here on earth.

Our faith helps us to answer the really difficult questions,

questions which, if left unanswered, can lead to despair, nihilism and sometimes even suicide. Questions like, 'Why are we here?' and 'What is the meaning of my life?'

An inability to answer such questions can leave people with a great emptiness at the heart of their lives, and that is why faith is such a gift. It enables those who have it to answer the truly important questions.

Our faith, as Catholics, reminds us that our obligations are universal to all humanity, not just to our own family or nation.

As Pope Pius XI reminded the world in 1922, even patriotism must be 'kept within the laws of Christ'. One of the laws of Christ is 'thou shalt not kill'.

And we must never think we know it all.

Our reason is a gift from God, and we must use it to examine our own lives, our faith and our failings – to examine our conscience, to use a very old-fashioned phrase. Perhaps if we did that more often, we would not need so many regulations and regulators.

The whole concept of human rights has a Christian root. If we believe God created each one of us, that provides us with a solid basis for respecting the human rights of all other people, who, as Christians, we believe were, whatever their faith, also created by God.

We thus have a solid and rational basis, for example, for respecting their right to life from conception to natural death, and also for helping to eliminate easily curable diseases, like malaria, that cause children to die prematurely. It is not enough to be pro-life for the unborn; we must be pro-life for the already born too, wherever they live.

We also have, in the recognition that we are all individually created by God, a rational basis for rejecting discrimination against people on the basis of who they are, the colour of their skin, or where they come from.

Above all, our faith tells us that we should follow the example of Christ and forgive others who have wronged us. Forgiveness is not something that comes naturally. In fact, it almost goes against nature. But we do it because we believe that Christ died so that we in our turn may be forgiven, and because He told us to forgive.

We must deplore the sin, but we should not shun the sinner.

Vengeance does not cure the injury to victims. Sometimes it makes it worse.

Retribution is not Christ's way. No, that hard and unnatural thing, *forgiveness*, is Christ's way.

It would help modern Ireland, with its now record-high prison population, if it could remind itself, this Easter, of the true meaning of Christ's life, and of the meaning of His death – forgiveness, letting go, and rising again.

Based on a short reflection I gave on what my faith means to me as a lay person in the Cathedral of Christ the King in Mullingar, Co. Westmeath on Holy Thursday evening, 5 April 2012.

SHOULD RELIGIOUS FORMATION BE PART OF THE SCHOOL DAY?

∞

In 2011, the then Minister for Education, Ruairi Quinn, was reported in the *Irish Independent*, to have said he would 'prefer if schools spent time improving reading and maths skills rather than preparing pupils for sacraments such as First Communion and Confirmation'.

He reportedly said that faith formation carried out during the day took up time that could be used in other ways, and referred in this context to the severe decline in performance by Irish pupils in the international OECD/PISA league table on literacy, dropping from 5th to 17th place, and he remarked that performance in maths had also fallen.

Primary school students spend thirty minutes per day on religion, which, in the case of Catholic schools, includes preparation for the sacraments.

Quinn said that while no person should enter the world without a clear knowledge and understanding of the history of religion, faith formation was a different thing. He said that faith formation 'takes up a lot of time' and that 'some people might suggest it might be done by parents or parish but outside school teaching hours'. He remarked that 'quite frankly, we have overloaded the curriculum'.

In contrast to what Quinn said, the actual rule governing schools says something completely different. It says: 'Of all the parts of a school curriculum Religious Instruction is by far the most important, as its subject-matter, God's honour and service, includes the proper use of all man's faculties, and affords the most powerful inducements to their proper use. Religious instruction is, therefore, a fundamental part of the school course, and a religious spirit should inform and vivify the whole work of the school.'

The present Minister for Education, Jan O'Sullivan, would like to revise this rule, presumably to give less prominence to religious teaching. Her department is preparing a White Paper (a government report giving concise information on an issue) on inclusivity which will propose new guidelines on how to manage children opting out of faith formation, especially in areas where they have no choice of school patronage.

For the White Paper, it has been proposed that faith formation classes be scheduled at the beginning or the end of the school day. It has also been suggested that children opting out of faith formation should have the benefit of an alternative class rather than being sent to a room for supervision. But it is not proposing the exclusion of religious formation from schools altogether, as was espoused by Ruairi Quinn.

The new arrangements will mean a debate about the relevance of religious education. So it is worth considering these issues.

Ruairi Quinn's more radical view deserves to be discussed, because there are many in the 'progressive' community who share it, and we can expect proposals like his, for totally non-denominational education excluding religion altogether, to re-emerge in coming years. The forthcoming changes to the rules will not be the last.

This is a debate about the proper content of education, of the content of preparation for citizenship. In that sense, it is a debate about who we think we are, or should be, as Irish people in the twenty-first century and beyond.

How are schools to be run? A two-hundred-year-old debate
There was very limited democratic political involvement in such debates in the past. As Seamus O'Buachalla said in his book, *Education Policy in the Twentieth Century* (Merlin, 1988): 'Parents, political parties and representatives of the socio-economic system have not figured as active participants in the policy process, the low level of involvement of the major parties is self-imposed.' That was true in 1988. It is still true today.

Dáil debates on education consisted, and still consist, largely of demands for more money for schooling, rather than discussions of what the schooling should be about.

The present structure of control of patronage or ownership of schools long predates the state itself. It has roots in the movement that led to Catholic Emancipation in 1829, and the reaction against the century-long religious settlement that had followed the end of the Williamite wars.

The present system of National Schools was launched in 1831, based on a proposal by a parliamentary committee chaired by Thomas Wyse MP, a Waterford man who was elected to represent Tipperary, and one of the first Catholics elected to the House of Commons. The first Board of Education was chaired by the Duke of Leinster, with clerical and lay representatives of different denominations present.

The idea put forward by Thomas Wyse was to provide combined literary, but separate religious, education. In other words, Protestant and Catholic children would go to the same schools, attend most classes together, but separate for religious instruction.

But the National Schools system did not remain multi-denominational for long.

According to Seamus O'Buachalla, the first objections came from the Church of Ireland. In 1832, a petition was lodged in Parliament by seventeen of the Church of Ireland bishops, protesting that the system deprived their clergy of their legal trust of superintending schools. This is not all that surprising in that, at that time, the Church of Ireland was still the state church.

Initially the Irish Catholic bishops had supported the National School system as proposed.

Archbishop Murray of Dublin actually became a member of the Board of Education. However, his pro-National education was opposed by the Archbishop of Tuam, Dr McHale, who has enjoyed, perhaps unjustifiably, a much better press from subsequent nationalist historians than has Dr Murray.

But Archbishop Murray's stance was also opposed by the Vatican. By 1841, Pope Gregory recognised that the operation of National Schools on a multi-denominational basis in the preceding ten years in Ireland had not, in fact, injured the Catholic religion, but ruled that participation by Catholics in multi-denominational National Schools should in future be decided by each local Catholic bishop. In practice, the bishops opted for denominational schools and this meant that the argument among Catholics went against multi-denominationalism.

By 1852, only 175 out of 4,795 National Schools were managed on a joint basis. Separating religious education from other aspects of the curriculum proved to be difficult in practice, especially as many of the teachers were themselves members of religious orders.

Nationalist opinion did not give much support to multi-denominational education either. In fact, separate education seems to have been what the people wanted at the time, and for more than a century thereafter. As remarked elsewhere in this book, Parnell was a strong supporter of separate denominational education.

With the benefit of hindsight, perhaps if Thomas Wyse's original idea had been adhered to, there might be fewer so-called peace walls keeping neighbours apart in Belfast today.

Should religious formation be removed from the school day?
Now I come to Ruairi Quinn's views. He was proposing more than just going back to Thomas Wyse's original model of common teaching of all subjects except religion. He was questioning whether religious formation should take place during the school day at all.

I agree with him that falling standards in Ireland's performance in OECD/PISA tests are profoundly discouraging. But where is the evidence that the thirty minutes per day spent on religion is responsible for this? As far as I know, that thirty minutes per day has not increased since the earlier tests in which Ireland obtained a creditable 5th place out of forty-one. So why single out religious formation? Why does Ruairi Quinn not, for example, refer to the teaching of a second language, Irish in most cases, on which I believe 120 minutes per day is spent? Perhaps because that has not increased either. Teaching two languages from the age of four is very demanding and is bound to squeeze out time for acquiring other competences.

Another possibility could be that the school year is too short. Irish second level (but not primary) schoolchildren spend slightly fewer hours per year in school than do their equivalents in the OECD as a whole. But that was also so when we got the earlier good result in the international comparison.

Of course, reducing the time spent on Irish would be very unpopular with some people. Increasing the length of the school year would be unpopular with others. But it was clearly wrong of Ruairi Quinn to single out the thirty minutes per day spent on religious formation, when there are so many other ways to find time to improve our scores in reading and mathematics.

It is also important not to enthrone results in OECD/PISA comparisons as the be-all-and-end-all of educational policy.

Education seeks to prepare children not just for working life, but for life as a whole. Education that focused narrowly on work available today would soon be obsolescent. The purpose of education is to develop the whole person – aesthetic, artistic, physical, moral, and spiritual. Furthermore, if people are believers in eternal life, religion is for them more important than other subjects.

Surely the school system should cater for them, if this is a pluralist country.

The minister has suggested that religious formation take place outside school hours. There are two possibilities here: that this be done in the evening or at the weekend. First, lets look at the home option.

While it is true that, in theory, under the Irish constitution the primary educator of the child is the family, in most households today both parents are also working in paid employment outside the home. Their working day usually ends later than does that of their children. To expect parents to make up, for the thirty minutes that might be lost to religious education during the school day, would be demanding.

A tired parent arrives home, prepares an evening meal, supervises homework for all non-religious subjects, and is then expected to give thirty minutes religious instruction after all that is done.

How realistic is that? How well qualified are most parents to do this? They may be observant in their own religious practice, but how prepared are they to become teachers?

Another possibility is to provide religious education in school, but not as part of the school day. Those who want religious education would either have to arrive at school half an hour early, or leave half an hour late. That would severely disrupt the school transport system, and would involve making significant demands on young children.

The other possibility would be that religious education be provided at the weekend, on a Saturday for example. To make up for the thirty minutes per day now provided would require two and a half hours' work. That would essentially mean that the children whose parents wanted them to have a religious education would have a five and a half day week, while other children would have a five day week. That would be a good way to kill off religious education altogether, which I am confident was not Ruairi Quinn's intention. Requiring religious education to take place at weekends would cut into time used for sport and exercise, and force parents to make a hard choice between faith formation and sport for their children.

It is important to say that many other matters, as well as reading mathematics and religion, are dealt with during the school day. Education in road safety, sport, positive health, nature study, and civics are all part of the school week. Nobody argues against that. Indeed there are frequent calls for a new topic to be added whenever a new social problem is identified that parents have no time to adequately cover.

If one argues that religion should be dealt with 'outside school hours', but that all these other non-core matters should continue to be dealt with at school, one is saying that religion is less important than road safety, sport, positive health, etc.

Given that, for many people, religion concerns itself with eternal life, that would be a pretty radical claim to make.

Should we follow the American model?
The argument may be made that in the United States religious education does not take place in public schools. And, despite that, there is a religiosity about American public life that is missing here.

Could such a system work here?

I do not believe it would. The United States is an immigrant society, and one where people move house far more often than they do in Europe. Churches provide a way of meeting people and integrating into a community, a role for churches that is less salient in European society.

There is also much more lively competition between churches in the United States. Half of all Americans change their religious affiliation during their lives.

The exclusion of religion from public schools has not helped the US get good grades in the OECD/PISA comparisons to which Ruairi Quinn referred.

US performance is much worse than Ireland's, and many American parents are prepared to pay very high fees to put their children into religiously run, or other private, schools in order to get them a decent education. As a result, the United States, originally a more egalitarian and meritocratic society than Europe, is rapidly becoming more socially stratified than Ireland is.

I would also add that the absence of religious education in schools in the United States may have contributed to an 'anything goes' approach to religious belief there, which puts the focus on what feels good rather than on what is true, and which allows some people who call themselves pastors to think it is a religious thing to burn the sacred books of other faiths.

An absence of religious formation in US public schools may also have contributed to a form of relativism which says 'believe what you like, it is of no interest to me', rather than a true pluralism which would say, 'I respect you and your convictions, because, like me, you too are seeking to find truth, to find out the meaning of our lives.'

Is faith formation a valid part of education?
But now I would like to turn to the wider question underlying the present debate: should there be faith formation at all? Is faith formation important for a society, or is it just a private matter?

I believe a religious sense is inherent in every human being. As G.K. Chesterton supposedly remarked, 'When a man stops believing in God he doesn't believe in nothing, he believes in anything.' Secular religions take the place of transcendental ones.

Communism, with its belief in iron laws of history and the ultimate utopia of a classless society, was a secular religion. Nazism, with its enthronement of race and its elaborate ritual, was another secular religion.

Once people ceased to believe that each human person was individually created by God, and thus had an inherent value that no other person had a right to take away, it became all too easy to accept concentration camps, gulags, ethnic cleansing and the elimination of class enemies. Other human lives just become objects, to be disposed of for the greater good, or the greater convenience of chosen lifestyles.

If there is no God, is there any basis for saying that there are any absolute values? In the absence of a sense of the *absolute*, what is a 'human right' in one generation could quite properly be deemed a luxury in another generation, and vice versa.

If we replace religion, what criterion will we use in determining what is 'good' and what is 'evil'?

What will guide our educational system in making moral judgements?

If society is not to descend into chaos it needs to develop a common sense of right and wrong. That is not something that will happen spontaneously. It has to be created through education, and through reasoning together.

Rabbi Jonathan Sacks described our modern dilemma thus: 'The idea of reasoning together was dealt a fateful blow in the twentieth century by the collapse of moral language, the disappearance of "I ought" and its replacement by "I want", "I choose", "I feel". Obligations can be debated. Wants, choices, and feelings can only be satisfied or frustrated.'

He went on to identify the importance of religion in providing a basis for the development of a shared civic sense of obligation, for each of our countries, and for our world.

He said: 'Reverence, restraint, humility, a sense of limits, the ability to listen and respond to human distress – these are not virtues produced by the market, yet they are attributes we will need if our global civilisation is to survive and they are an essential part of the religious imagination.'

Those who would banish religious formation from our schools should reflect on those words of the former Chief Rabbi of Great Britain.

Are there adequate alternatives to religion as a source for a social ethic? Of course, people who believe religious formation does not belong in schools may argue that there are other sources to draw upon in shaping the ethics of children.

Could not science, material progress, freedom, a secular ethic, or human rights perform that role? Could a combination of these provide us with a sufficient sense of what is good and what is evil, so that we could safely banish religious belief to the private sphere, as something unnecessary to the formation of future citizens?

Science, as we know, is a search for truth, but on its own it has no inherent ethical boundaries. The application of science has given us marvellous medical advances, improved sanitation, and wonderful new means of communication. But it has also given us the atom bomb, the depletion of scarce water resources, and climate change.

Material progress has not been cost free. Beyond a certain point, which we in Ireland passed about thirty years ago, there seems to be no correlation between improvement in average material living standards and improved wellbeing. This is a finding of economists who have been studying the 'economics of happiness'.

The same economic studies suggest that, when it comes to links between material wealth and a sense of wellbeing, wellbeing comes from feeling better off than those with whom we habitually compare ourselves, rather than on absolute levels of material wealth.

If we can afford a better car than our brother-in-law, we feel well off. If all we can afford is a cheaper one, we feel worse off. Thus it becomes an endless and unsatisfying struggle.

A religious sense, if it is allowed to develop, would put all these things back into proportion.

Should freedom be the goal? Should we just leave it to people to decide for themselves how to use their freedom, without any collective communal guidance?

The trouble with 'freedom' as a goal for society is that it is a purely individualistic concept. It says nothing about how we should treat other people. It would, for example, validate the pursuit of private profit regardless of the effect that has on other people, or on the environment.

Freedom can only exist in the framework of law, otherwise it becomes chaos. And lawmaking involves value judgements, and the values underlying law have to come from a source above and beyond the law itself. Otherwise law is just a malleable thing based on popular consensus and majority opinion, which as we know is highly fickle and contingent on emotional waves. Majorities can be both blind and unjust, at times.

Can ethics be separated from religion?
I think it is difficult to come up with a complete set of ethical principles without having an opinion on the purpose of human life, why we are here, and who we are as humans.

Some would argue that we can have a concept of human rights that is entirely separate from our concept of how each human being came into existence, of the value of human life, and of whether that life exists in any continuing form after death. I believe Christians could reach a wide level of agreement on a lot of human rights topics with people who believed this, but not complete agreement. Why do I say that?

Genomics, the science of genes, brings us up against the limits of such an approach. Is it okay to 'create' a new, better man, with fewer diseases, in a test tube, to experiment with human beings, to discard some and retain others? I believe these are questions that go beyond any possibility of absolute determination by some system of secular, religion free, ethics.

When do we become sufficiently 'human' to have human rights?

Are human rights inherent from the beginning of life, or are they contingent on whether we can live independently, as some might argue? These issues cannot be decided for us by science on its own.

In the absence of a scientific answer, the question is left to politics. And, as we know from the debate about abortion in other countries, the best politics can come up with is some arbitrary rule, determined by a temporary political compromise.

That shows the limits of the human rights model on its own, if it is separated from a deeper consensus on the nature and meaning of human life.

A similar problem of agreeing on common assumptions arises in a dialogue on human rights with countries like China, whose Marxist materialist ideology and Confucian ethic give it a different view on the value of individual lives.

Islamic societies would also have different priorities than western societies, whose 'secular' notions of human rights have roots in, often unremembered, unacknowledged and diluted Christian assumptions.

I believe the cultivation of a religious sense, through religious education, is a vital part of education. Education is about more than facts. It is about learning how to live, how to make judgements. Anyone who sets out to educate children and prepare them for life, and for making judgements, has to start with their own belief of what constitutes a good life and good judgement. I think that is self-evident.

So I think it follows that teachers need to believe what they are teaching and schools do need to have a shared belief system.

Faith and reason are compatible
Of course this does not mean that religion should have free rein, without critical rational challenge.

Without a constant questioning, faith can become a form of oppression, a fanaticism that distorts our humanity. As Pope Benedict XVI said in his famous Regensburg address, there is a proper dialogue that must always go on between faith and reason. They should influence one another constantly. Religion must check the hubris of faith, and faith that of reason.

As he said before he became Pope, in a speech in Saint Etienne in June 2004: 'I would say that there can be no peace in the world without genuine peace between reason and faith, because without peace between reason and religion, the sources of morality and law dry up.'

So I would argue that faith formation does have a place in our schools, a place that it should share peacefully with science, literacy, mathematics and all those other good things.

Based on a speech delivered as part of the 'Lenten lectures' series, 7 April 2011, Radisson Hotel, Dublin

THE CHURCHES AND THE EUROPEAN UNION

What should the relationship be between the churches and the European Union?

Secularists might claim that there should be no such relationship, that the European Union is a political institution for all the people and that, as such, it should operate in an entirely separate sphere from that of the churches. They would say that churches should neither influence, nor be influenced by, political institutions. They would say that political institutions should remain strictly secular, not only in their form, but also in the influences upon them.

I believe this secularist view to be naive in its understanding of human nature for a number of reasons.

Firstly, voters do not divide their minds up into watertight compartments marked 'religious', 'political', 'personal', 'family' and so forth. What goes on in one part of their mind influences what goes on in all the others.

Secondly, no one will deny that ethical beliefs can, and should, influence the actions of political institutions, whether that be at national, local or European level. It would be very difficult to separate people's ethical beliefs from the religious source from which many people's ethics spring. So if ethics influences politics, religious belief will also influence it.

That is not to claim that people with no religious belief have no ethical beliefs – of course they do, often very strong and considered ones – but it is to say that those who have religious beliefs do draw heavily on their religious heritage and practice in formulating these beliefs, and more importantly in holding themselves accountable for how they follow them.

Thirdly, humans are social beings. They do not live atomised lives. They live in multiple overlapping communities of families, neighbourhoods, workplaces, political parties, nations, sports clubs, and for many, in the community of a church.

The ethos of society is formed, in varying degrees, in all of these communities. And without a shared ethos of some kind, it would be very difficult for any society to function. In varying degrees, the shared ethos of each European society has been formed over the years by (among other things) the religious beliefs of some or all of its citizens, and by the thought those citizens gave to these beliefs when they came together in churches, meeting houses and mosques. And they continue, in those venues, to reflect on those beliefs, and hold themselves accountable for how well they live up to them.

Laws are obeyed not only out of fear of retribution, but just as importantly out of this sense of a shared ethos; an ethos that forms a basis for trust, an ethos that thus makes government and governance possible. It is impossible to completely disentangle this shared ethos from the heritage of religious belief, or unbelief.

Therefore I suggest that as long as religious belief exists, and there is every reason to believe it will always exist, a secularist notion that religion and politics should be kept entirely separate is simply unrealistic, even naive. And naive beliefs pursued relentlessly, as they often are, lead towards either tyranny or the breakdown of the pluralism that is required if democracy is to function.

People of faith are part of society, and they deserve to be able, in the exercise of pluralism, to bring their beliefs unashamedly into the public sphere just as much as people of other belief systems are entitled to do.

Of course, secularism did not appear out of thin air. It was a reaction to an excessive and immoderate intertwining of religion and politics in the past. But secularists should now beware of committing the same errors of immoderation today, that they justly condemn churches for in the past.

For example, to seek to use the power of the state to remove every symbol or sign of religious belief from the public space would be just as immoderate as past efforts to use the powers of the state to push one religion on people.

It is worth recalling too that the European Convention on Human Rights, approved in 1949 before the EU came into existence, guarantees every European the right, in its words, to 'manifest his religion, with others in public or private, in teaching, practice, worship and observance'.

This right to manifest religious belief is not subordinate to other rights in the Convention.

The Convention must be read as a whole. And the EU submits itself to the whole Convention, including the article in the Lisbon Treaty about how people may exercise their religious freedom. It is right, of course, to point out that the Convention extends its protection to all religions and not just to Christianity.

In that context, it appears to me that the Swiss vote to ban minarets on mosques in Switzerland is a denial of the right to 'manifest' religious belief 'in public' as guaranteed by the Convention. Likewise, Christians should not confuse Christianity with some form of Eurocentric cultural or ethnic nationalism. Christians believe that Christ came down to earth to save all mankind, not just people who can prove European ancestry.

I hope I have shown that it is not possible to entirely separate the religion practised by a significant body of its members or citizens from any political entity such as the European Union, or vice versa. But there are, of course, clear distinctions of function which must be respected.

Working out these boundaries will be an unending negotiation, and the boundaries will shift slightly from time to time. That there will be a continuing argument about the exact boundary should be accepted, and should not be seen as threatening on either side. In the past, churches took on roles that the state was unwilling or unable to take on. Some of these can now more easily be performed by the state, with its increased resources, and in light of the reduced full-time manpower available to the churches.

But there are areas the state should not enter, and areas that the churches should leave to secular authorities. As the Lisbon Treaty puts it, in Article 17, the Union 'respects and does not prejudice the status under national law of churches' and 'shall maintain open, transparent and regular dialogue with these churches'.

Now that the Lisbon Treaty is in force, that dialogue is formally required of the Union.

Such dialogue would only make sense if the Union was open to be influenced by the churches. What other purpose would the dialogue have? It is important to ensure that both the Union and the churches take the new obligations in the treaty seriously.

I am aware that the President of the European Commission, the President of the European Council and the Vice-President of the European Parliament have already had a formal dialogue with the churches and philosophical organisations, on 10 June 2014, pursuant to Article 17 of the treaties. (Agenda items can be raised by either side. Forty-three religious and philosophical organisations have registered to be eligible to take part.)

While the EU institutions have an obligation to respect the independent sphere of action of religious organisations, churches have a similar obligation to respect duly constituted political institutions exercising their proper functions.

Churches should not take over the role of a state, or its citizens, but they can help them discern what to do, and have the patient commitment to carry it through.

Recently the Catholic bishops of the EU identified the core motivation of the Schuman Declaration (the declaration on 9 May 1950 of the French Foreign Minister which led to the establishment of the European Union), as being 'essentially an appeal for mutual forgiveness', and as such it is a profoundly Christian act, a Christian duty too, but one too often neglected in relations between states and nations. I know that one will find similar sentiments in the doctrines of other religions in Europe.

Forgiveness is a key word here. It is all too easy to demand apologies relating to a historical wrong committed against one nation, but rarely does one hear calls for full and final forgiveness to be granted by the offended party.

Indeed the 'name and shame' culture, shaped by modern media competition, seems to leave little space for forgiveness.

But it was mutual forgiveness that was the unique element in the formation of the European Union. That point seems lost on some nowadays.

The formation of the European Union was also driven by an impulse of solidarity; solidarity between European states and between the people of Europe, a solidarity not confined within national frontiers.

As Pope Benedict XVI put it in his encyclical, *Caritas in Veritate* (2009): 'Without internal forms of solidarity and mutual trust, the market cannot completely fulfil its proper economic function. And today it is this trust that has ceased to exist, and the loss of trust is a great loss.'

This is a very important insight into economics. All markets depend on trust. Without trust, we would find ourselves spending so much on lawyers that trading with one another would become incredibly expensive.

But where does trust come from? It comes from a shared ethos or belief system. And where, for many people, does their ethos come from? To a significant degree, it comes from their religious beliefs or heritage.

National, European and international regulations alone cannot create the degree of trust and confidence necessary for markets to function. There has to be trust too. Ask business people about doing business in China today and they will tell you about great opportunities there that are severely mitigated by symptoms of lack of trust, such as corruption and intellectual property theft.

To summarise, this is what churches contribute to the processes of the European Union:

- An understanding of the project's moral and spiritual roots,
- An insight into the mutual trust necessary to build a common market,
- The patience and wisdom that comes from being a 2,000-year-old institution, and,
- A perspective on our responsibility towards future generations yet unborn.

These are strengths on which Europeans can draw. They threaten nobody. They diminish nobody. They are not all of what Europe is about, but they are an important part of it.

Based on a speech given in April 2010, at the invitation of my friend Gay Mitchell MEP, to the Human Dignity Group in the European Parliament.

MICHAEL FOGARTY MEMORIAL LECTURE

༄

I believe Christian democracy is just as relevant today as it was when Michael Fogarty studied Catholic Social Thinking in the 1930s, when he worked in the Economic and Social Research Institute in Dublin from 1967 to 1973, and later on when he served as chairman of Oxfordshire County Council.

Politics should be open to influence by people of faith. Getting involved in politics is one of the best ways to promote Christian values. Opting out of political life, in an effort to recreate a romanticised past, leads nowhere.

Why should politics be influenced by people of faith?

His Holiness Pope Benedict XVI summed it all up very well, when, during his Westminster visit, he said: 'I would suggest that the world of reason and the world of faith – the world of secular rationality and the world of religious belief – need one another and should not be afraid to enter into a profound and ongoing dialogue, for the good of our civilisation. Religion, in other words, is not a problem for legislators to solve, but a vital contributor to the national conversation.'

As long as religious belief exists, and there is every reason to believe it will always exist, the secularist notion that religion and politics should be kept entirely separate is simply unrealistic.

One of the major challenges we have to work on today, as Christian democrats, is the relationship in mixed societies between Christianity and Islam. As the then Archbishop of Canterbury, Rowan Williams said, in a speech on Christian/Muslim relations, 'both our faiths are missionary faiths ... precisely because we have that in common, it is not easy to find a space we can inhabit together'.

Yet, as he also pointed out, we share a passion for universal truth, and that helps us to recognise in one another the same fundamental seriousness about the most important issues.

I believe that Christian democracy, which is founded not on individualism but on respect for the fundamental value of each person, is well placed to help society respect the fundamental value of each Muslim person in every respect, including in his or her religious beliefs.

I would also argue that Christian churches, precisely because they are religious institutions, are better placed to reach out to believing Muslims in a respectful way, through common activities at local level. Christian-democrat inspired political parties should also be open to the membership of non-Christians who accept the social principles we seek to put into action through politics.

Having made the case that Christian believers have a right to bring their religious insights to bear on political questions, I would now like to say how these insights can help find answers to some of the political questions of our day.

I will start with the economic problems of the Western world – economic problems that have been brought to the surface by the financial crisis, but which existed already anyway.

The credit boom in some Western countries since 2000, which was fuelled by Chinese, Japanese and German savings, was an anaesthetic that prevented the symptoms of underlying problems from emerging.

In that sense, we would have been better off if the crisis had occurred sooner, because we would then have been forced to deal with the underlying problems sooner, and less painfully.

The underlying problems are:

- The ageing of our societies,
- The way our education systems fail some of our children,
- The unsustainability of western patterns of energy and food consumption,
- The distorted allocation of resources in capital markets, and,
- Our inadequate means of supervising the flow of capital across borders.

The fact that people are living longer has meant that the pension systems of most western countries are unviable. People are now retired for too long a period to be supported by the contributions they made in taxation or to pension schemes during their working lives. This was made worse by mistaken early-retirement schemes introduced to create jobs for younger people, or to solve short-term public finance difficulties.

The emphasis that Christians place on the family, and the bonds that unite families, will become more important as the welfare state, to which many family responsibilities were transferred in the past sixty years, becomes financially less capable of bearing them.

The ageing of societies has also contributed, along with medical negligence cases and incentives to overuse drugs and tests, to an explosion in health costs. The United States is the worst case here but other countries are heading in the same direction.

These problems were known during the credit boom, but little was done about them because money was plentiful – artificially so. Anyone who proposed unpopular changes at that time would have been accused of being a heartless bookkeeper.

Education systems have also been failing to respond to challenges. A significant proportion of young people continue to drop out of school with few or no qualifications. The only jobs some of them are qualified to do are ones that can be done cheaply in Vietnam or China.

The educational system has been designed for those with academic aptitudes, but not to nurture other forms of intelligence. This is a failure of imagination and intellect by educationalists, rather than just a failure to provide money. An education system which caters well for those who can compete academically, but has no relevant answers for those whose talents lie in other directions, is not living up to the Christian democrat motto that 'every person counts'.

Young unqualified males are particularly vulnerable. 75% of the recently unemployed in the US are male. Young females may find jobs locally in the service sector, but the jobs that unskilled males used to do have either migrated to the Far East, or were in volatile sectors, like construction.

Globalisation gave great rewards to those who had the skill to position themselves at the busy crossroads of the information society, like in finance, entertainment, law, or professional sport, where they could either levy what economists call an 'economic rent' (i.e. an artificial scarcity premium) on the rest of society, or could hold their employer to ransom by threatening to move to another firm, or to another jurisdiction with a lower tax rate.

But globalisation has left other people behind. It has, of course, brought lower prices and increased consumer choice, but the benefits have not always been distributed fairly. Fairness can be a nebulous concept. It can also be a cover for self-serving arguments.

As I see it, fairness is not a matter of looking for equalisation of incomes. Fairness is a matter of looking for financial returns proportionate

- To the effort people put in,
- To the risks they have taken,
- To talent they have, and,
- To the social contribution they are making.

This is all a matter of judgement based on values.

Fairness cannot be achieved by a state-imposed incomes policy, as was attempted in Britain and many other countries in the 1970s. But it can be brought about if long-term values get a better hearing in the boardrooms of companies, and by the enforcement of competition policies that make it harder to charge 'economic rent'.

Economic activity is a means to an end. The end we seek is a society at ease with itself because every member of society feels that his or her contribution is respected.

The financial crisis has also laid bare the fundamental unsustainability of our patterns of energy and food consumption in the Western World.

There is not enough oil, nor enough fertile land, nor enough unpolluted atmosphere in the world to cater for a situation in which Indians, Chinese and Brazilians consume oil, coal, and livestock products at the rate we do in Europe and America.

It takes far more acres to produce protein and calories off the back of an animal than straight from the ground in an edible crop.

The legacy of colonial intervention in China and India held those countries back for two centuries. Western patterns of consumption of food and energy only became possible in the first place because there was less competition for these resources from those countries, and because Western countries, for about a century and a quarter starting in 1850, controlled the rules of the economic game. That era is now over.

The growing middle classes in emerging economies will look for the same energy usage, and meat- and dairy-intensive diets, that we in the West take for granted. Energy and food prices will inevitably rise because of that. On present trends, China's oil imports will double in the next twenty years.

The capital markets have not covered themselves in glory in recent years either. Thanks to financial innovations, shares in companies could be bought and sold with much greater frequency than ever before. Hostile takeovers were easier to mount. This meant that companies were judged, and executives rewarded, on the basis of very short-term movements of share prices.

This had its most devastating effect in banking, where credit broke down completely in 2008.

And what is credit after all? Credit is trust. That is what the word means. All markets depend on trust. Markets need ethics, and, for many, ethics derive from religious belief.

In 2008, we had to save the banking system. Over the last four centuries banking allowed us to use our resources in ways that would have been impossible without it. But, in the medium term, we also need to decide the proper role, function, and scale of banking in our society.

We need a banking policy, not just a bank rescue policy. Banks that are 'too big to be allowed to fail' or 'too interconnected to be allowed to fail' must never again drag taxpayers unwittingly into underwriting huge private risks.

The short-termism that brought banking down infected other businesses too. Productivity gains were preferred to innovations. The human capital of a company was valued less than it should be.

We are only beginning to consider how to change this. One suggestion is to enhance the voting rights of shareholders who hold their shares in a company for a longer period.

The freeing up of global capital markets has outdistanced the supervisory capacity, and even the understanding, of national financial regulators.

Politically created problems need political solutions. The venue in which these political solutions should be found is the G20. But the G20 has not yet fully found its feet, and is governed by a rotating presidency, something the EU has found to be unsatisfactory.

In fact, if free movement of capital across borders is to continue, the world needs to establish a system of cross-border economic governance that highlights imbalances and distortions, long before they become bubbles about to burst.

Fines and penalties may not be necessary. So long as information is shared and published in a timely way, intelligently guided markets should discipline delinquent behaviour.

The job of supervisors and rating agencies is to ensure that the information is obtained and published in good time and is interpreted intelligently and courageously. That did not happen in recent times, and rating agencies were entangled in unethical conflicts of interest, which compromised their integrity. The IMF should be given the full range of supervisory functions over all its members, including the United States and China.

Markets need rules, and the rules must be enforced. The market is a social and legislative construct. If the absence of rules and untrammelled freedom was the best way to a good market economy, Somalia would be the richest country in the world!

But even if we do all these things right, as I have said earlier, I believe we are entering a period where material conditions for western countries will (in relative but hopefully not absolute terms) not be as good as they were.

Our share of the world's wealth will be less.

The West's ability to control the rules of the game will be less too. We will no longer be able to keep tariffs high for things like textiles and cotton to protect our own producers, while insisting that tariffs are low for what we want to export.

We will also have pensions to pay, debts to repay, and a diminishing workforce to earn the money needed to do so.

Compared to our grandparents, we will remain very wealthy,

but compared to people in other parts of the world, we will be comparatively less well off than we are today.

I maintain that religious belief will help us put these changes into proper proportion. It will help us realise that material progress is not, and never was, the elixir of happiness.

A survey a few years ago found that the Japanese were ten times better off financially than the Poles, but no happier. The Poles were happier than the Hungarians, despite similar levels of wealth. The United States today is much richer than it was in 1960, but the divorce rate has doubled, the prison population has increased fivefold, and clinical depression has tripled. People there are richer, but no happier than they were in 1960.

This is not to say that material wealth does not bring happiness to nations. Up to a certain average per capita wealth, it does. But above that level, and we are already far above that level in most western European countries, it seems to make little difference, on average.

Unfortunately, studies suggest that what makes people relatively happier is not so much being better off, as being relatively better off than whoever they normally compare themselves with. And conversely, what makes them unhappy is falling behind those people.

What people really want, and need, is a sense of control over their own lives, and a sense of belonging.

Sometimes, accepting that we have enough is key to a good life. That may not please the economists who are constantly looking around for 'consumer confidence' – a barren and soulless concept if ever there was one!

So, in the end, the economic problem is one of values.

The values we need to survive the recession are ones that bring us out of ourselves, that help us to transcend our own problems, by caring about others, and by giving service to something greater than ourselves.

It is noteworthy how the recession is altering people's values already.

The chief executive of the Society of St Vincent de Paul in Ireland told me that his organisation have been able to set up more conferences (branches), with new volunteers, during the recession than it had been able to do in the previous twenty years.

As Pope Benedict XVI put it when he spoke in Prague in 2011, 'Human aspirations soar beyond the self, beyond what any political or economic authority can provide, towards a radiant hope that has its origin beyond ourselves yet is encountered within, as truth and beauty and goodness.'

Based on the Michael Fogarty Lecture of December 2012, given in the House of Lords, at the invitation of Lord Alton and the UK Movement for Christian Democracy. The late Michael Fogarty, who worked for a time in Ireland, was recognised as one of the foremost historians and thinkers on Christian democracy writing in the English language. The Fogarty Lecture is sponsored by the Centre for Christian Democracy, which is affiliated with the European People's Party. I was Vice-President of the European People's Party from 1992 to 2005.

ST PATRICK

∽

The life of St Patrick holds very important lessons for us now in the twenty-first century.

St Patrick was, above all, a Christian man of faith. His faith was so deep that he was prepared to go back among a people who had previously enslaved him to share that faith, that good news, with them.

He did not do it for material wealth. He did it because of belief in a cause, a reality greater than himself, greater than all humankind. I believe that faith, and a consequential willingness to work for a greater cause, is something we need to rediscover, and foster, in this generation.

St Patrick was born Welsh or British, and a citizen of the Roman Empire, a Roman Empire that encompassed most of Western Europe and the Near East. But by the time he died, the Roman Empire had fallen, Rome itself had been taken, and Europe did not rediscover its unity until modern times.

Irish people should remember where St Patrick came from. If, as is likely, he had brothers and sisters, their distant descendants are probably living today in Wales, the South West or the North West of England. This reminds us of how much our two islands, Ireland and Britain, have in common. It reminds us of the good things we have given to one another, and continue to give to this day.

Perhaps even more topically, in these anxious economic times, we should reflect on what happened to the economy of Northern Europe during St Patrick's lifetime.

When he was born there was considerable prosperity, a common currency system for all of Europe, based on silver coinage minted in the name of the Roman Empire. This currency, this means of exchange, enabled citizens of Rome, including St Patrick's family, to trade across long distances, to buy and sell goods, and probably to enjoy a good standard of living.

By the time St Patrick died, this system had collapsed.

Because it was cut off from Rome, silver was no longer available in Britain to provide currency, and there was no longer any political authority strong enough to stand behind an alternative currency. As a result, scholars now believe that living standards in post-Roman Britain fell dramatically, to perhaps a quarter of their previous level, and stayed at that level for centuries. All during the lifetime of St Patrick.

This shows the fragility of all economic systems, how dependent they are on political conditions, and how change can be sudden and destructive, as well as slow and benign.

While St Patrick had his mind on other, arguably much more important, things, we can learn a lot from what happened to the economy during his life.

We need to be careful to value and maintain a political system that encourages trade, sustains credit, and keeps all of us open to the needs and aspirations of people far away from us, and very different from us, as different as the Irish who captured and enslaved St Patrick as a boy must have seemed to him at the time.

In a word, economics and finance are important, but they are dependent on a robust, believable and strong political system; something that existed when St Patrick was born, but had disappeared by the time he had died.

Based on a speech I gave on 17 March 2011, at the dinner of the Friendly Sons of St Patrick in Scranton, Pennsylvania. It was a tremendously enjoyable night, at which I forged some enduring friendships. I was deeply honoured to be invited to address this dinner, an honour that has also been given to three other former Taoiseach of Ireland: Garret FitzGerald, Albert Reynolds and Bertie Ahern. Others who have spoken at this dinner include President Harry Truman, Senator Robert Kennedy, Senator Hubert Humphrey, Senator Eugene McCarthy, Senator Bob Casey, and Governors Bill Scranton and Martin O'Malley.

EUCHARISTIC CONGRESS 2012

∞

According to Pope Benedict, anyone who 'in search of truth, trusts only his individual actions, and does not recognise the help of others, is deceiving himself'.

In this light, I would like to look at what the Eucharist means in the modern world, what it might tell us about how we should live our lives, in families, in local communities, and about how we should engage in politics.

It all starts with the Eucharist

Catholic Christianity is Eucharistic Christianity. For the Catholic in the street, so to speak, it all starts with the Eucharist. The Second Vatican Council put it this way: 'The Eucharist is the *source* and *summit* of Christian life ... it casts light on how we are to live.'

The very word 'Communion' means a coming together of people.

The words said at the consecration in the Mass, 'This is my body', 'This is my blood', and the invitation to take and eat, to receive Christ into ourselves, are found in St Paul's first letter to the Corinthians in Chapter 12.

In St Paul's letter, these words, used in the consecration every day, are immediately preceded by a reproof to the Corinthians about the way they had started to celebrate the Lord's Supper in Corinth.

The Lord's Supper, in Corinth as elsewhere, was as a common meal, to be eaten together by all the faithful. But divisions had grown up among the Christians of Corinth. Because of these divisions, some better-off members of the Christian community in Corinth did not want to share their food with others. St Paul had learned that they went ahead and ate, without waiting for all – especially for the less well-off – to arrive and take part.

St Paul had no time for that. He said, 'Have you no respect for the church of God, and would you humiliate those who have nothing? … Shall I commend you? In this matter I do not commend you,' deploring the Corinthians lack of community and mutual respect – their lack of *communion* – in the way they celebrated the Eucharist.

Later in his letter to the Corinthians, just a paragraph or two after the words of the consecration, St Paul called on the Corinthians to examine their consciences.

He said, 'But let a person look carefully at himself and in that spirit eat the bread and drink the cup,' and later adds, 'If, however, we scrutinise ourselves, we should not be judged.'

In the Catholic Eucharist, the emphasis is, of course, on the presence of Christ in the celebration, the transubstantiation of the bread and wine on the altar into the body and blood of Christ, a belief that is central to our faith. Indeed it is a conviction so radical that, if we truly accept it, it *must* change our lives.

Communion with other people: an approach to politics
The Eucharist, and Christianity, is all about the quality of our relationship with each other. Is it a relationship of trust and respect, or is it something else?

The absence of trust and respect in the relationship between Christian nations was forcibly rediscovered in the violent first half of the twentieth century.

To formulate this in terms of the Eucharistic Congress, Eucharist is communion with Christ *and* with one another.

From reading the full text of his letter to the Corinthians we can see the emphasis he puts on the unifying power of the Eucharist when he reminded the Corinthians of the words Jesus had used at the Last Supper. Words which are still repeated every day at the consecration of the Mass.

That is where the link can be made between the Eucharist and politics and political institutions. Politics is one of the ways by which Catholics, Christians and people of faith generally, come together with other people. Is the relationship we forge with one another through politics, one of justice and respect, or does it fall into some of the errors of disputatiousness and class division that St Paul found among the faithful living in the city of Corinth?

Likewise, do we feel free to bring some of the sense of justice and mutual respect we gain from sharing the Eucharist to bear in politics for the benefit of the wider community?

A sense of proportion in politics
What is the 'added value', to use a piece of business jargon, that Christians can bring to politics?

Faith in eternal life helps one to be humble in all things – including in one's contribution to politics – to accept that we do not know it all. Because our faith tells us that there is a God, that we are not alone in the universe, we should not be arrogant. Just as our religious life should be an endless pursuit of a truth we will never fully know, so should our political life be.

We should not act as if this generation, with all its technologies, has all the answers. Faith tells us that, no matter how hard we try, we are not going to create a heaven on earth, and that totalitarian or materialist philosophies that pretend to do so are just plain wrong. But faith also tells us that there is such a thing as fundamental truth, for which we must seek, using our reason and informed by the teachings of Jesus Christ.

Fundamental truths and fundamental rights
If we believe there are certain fundamental truths, then we cannot claim that what is right or wrong, what is true or untrue, is to be determined solely by the political consensus in a society at a particular time.

Opinion polls are not the determinant of truth, nor, for that matter, is the 'latest scientific research'. Opinion polls are just opinion polls, and research is just research. Both can and will be superseded by other polls and further research. Meanwhile fundamental truths remain true.

Truth and right are not contingent. Majorities can be wrong, and often are. As the then Cardinal Ratzinger put it in a chapter of his collected writings, entitled *The Problem of the Threats to Human Life*: 'In a world in which moral convictions lack a common reference to the truth, such convictions have the value of mere opinion.'

In that, Christianity is in agreement with the approach of the framers of the Universal Declaration of Human Rights, who also held that there were certain fundamentals that were antecedent to the opinion of the majority at any given time.

A belief in the existence of fundamental truths underlies any viable concept of fundamental rights. If one believed everything was relative, and nothing was fundamental, it would be hard to discern which rights were fundamental and which rights should simply be contingent on particular circumstances. There is a deep-seated tension in modern society between the widespread belief that everything is relative, and the idea that certain rights of human beings are fundamental and should *not* be seen as relative.

Conscience
In approaching political questions, a Christian must be influenced by his or her conscience, just as St Paul recommended we should be when participating in the Eucharist.

Our reason is a gift from God, and we must use it to examine our own lives, our faith and our failings. Perhaps a more frequent public and private examination of conscience by individuals and organisations would reduce the need for so many regulations and regulators. As St Paul said to the Corinthians, 'If we scrutinise ourselves, we should not be judged.'

I have, in some of the work I have been doing in business, come across some excellent work on how best to promote ethical behaviour in large business organisations. In a real sense, it is a systematic application of what St Paul recommended so long ago.

Our faith, and our conscience, also tells us we should respect God's creation. We should leave the earth in a better condition than we found it. That should influence our politics.

Every person counts
I think the whole concept of human rights has a Christian root, which can be expressed in the phrase 'every person counts'. If we believe God created each one of us as individuals, it is easy to understand why we should respect the human rights of all other people, each of whom we believe has also been individually created by God. That is why every person counts.

A belief that we are each a creation of God makes it reasonable to respect the right to life from conception to natural death, and, equally importantly, to help eliminate easily curable diseases, like malaria, that cause children to die prematurely. Just because a human being has not yet been born, or lives out of our sight on another continent, does not mean that there is no call on us to vindicate their human rights. It is not a question of taking a moralistic position, but rather a question of what we do, and how we live our lives.

Our faith tells us that there is a life after our death; we do not simply pass away into nothingness. We have to give an account of ourselves.

Forgiveness
Our faith also tells us that God sent His only Son to live, and die, on Earth, so that our sins would be forgiven and that we might live. Our faith tells us that we should follow the example of Christ and forgive others who have wronged us.

Penalties are necessary to ensure that laws are respected, and may involve terms of imprisonment, but these penalties should be calculated in accordance with the need for deterrence and restitution, not as a form vengeance or catharsis for victims. And once a penalty is paid, offenders should be forgiven.

I will back up this point by quoting from a recent article by Michael Gerson in the *Washington Post* on the death of former Watergate convict, Chuck Colson. After imprisonment for the obstruction of justice, Colson went on to devote his life to Christianity and to the improvement of prison conditions: 'Prison often figures large in conversion stories. Pride is the enemy of grace, and prison the enemy of pride.' 'How else but through a broken heart may Lord Christ enter in?' wrote Oscar Wilde after his release from Reading Gaol.

Gerson concluded, 'It is the central paradox of Christianity that fulfilment starts in emptiness, that streams emerge in the desert, that freedom can be found in a prison cell.'

Globalisation and inequality
These are some of the insights that Christianity can bring to political life.

Christian belief is, I contend, as important to the living of a good life now, in the twenty-first century in Ireland, as it ever was at any time in our country's long history.

It is also important to understanding how best to live in a globalised world. In his encyclical *Caritas in Veritate* (2009), speaking of the world economy, Pope Benedict XVI said, 'The principal new feature has been the explosion of worldwide interdependence, commonly known as globalisation.'

He went on to say that, without the guidance of charity in truth, globalisation could cause unprecedented damage and create new divisions in the human family. He is right.

Thanks in part to globalisation, modern western society is afflicted by growing inequality in incomes, reversing a period of relative equalisation following the Second World War.

Money and talent can now move more freely than ever before across frontiers, and this reduces the possibility of individual states using progressive taxation to mitigate inequalities of income between people.

Remuneration policies within companies are also driven by the fear that 'talent' will be stolen by competitors. This can lead to big differences between what people at the top of a company can earn, and what is earned by others, who are less well known and less likely to be headhunted by competitors.

To change this will require a change in the ethic by which capitalism operates.

That is something that can be influenced for good by religious ethical principles, whether these principles are applied in government, in company boardrooms, or among the investment community, or even by individuals in their daily lives, as shoppers, voters, or as contributors to public debate.

Trust and respect
No Christian, and Catholics in particular, should be afraid to bring their beliefs into the public square.

Drawing on their faith, they can help society to work out, and maintain, a strong ethos of mutual trust and respect,

- Within religious communities,
- Between religious communities,
- Between people of faith and non-believers,
- In business and economic relations, and,
- Between nations.

That is what we have to offer the twenty-first century, and we should be putting it forward with pride.

Based on the speech I was asked to give at the Eucharistic Congress in June 2012 at the RDS, Dublin. This was a rare honour. The Congress had last been held in Dublin in 1932. It is a gathering of Catholics from all over the world. Apart from the religious ceremonies, the Congress consisted of a series of workshops, and I had the privilege of speaking at one.